TOTALLY
COMMITTED!

The Importance of Commitment
in Biblical Teaching

TOTALLY COMMITTED!

The Importance of Commitment in Biblical Teaching

Revised Edition

Eric H.H. Chang

Revised by Bentley C.F. Chan

Totally Committed! The Importance of Commitment in Biblical Teaching
By Eric H.H. Chang, Revised by Bentley C.F. Chan

Copyright © 2001, 2015
Eric H.H. Chang, Helen Chang, Bentley C.F. Chan

ISBN-13: 978-1515071686
ISBN-10: 1515071685

Printed in the United States of America
by CreateSpace, an Amazon.com company
Charleston, South Carolina, USA

Print edition available from Amazon.com and other online stores
Kindle e-book available at Kindle and online stores

Cover design by Bentley C.F. Chan
Upper cover photo © Can Stock Photo Inc. / rozum
Lower cover photo © Mikadun / Shutterstock

Contents

Dedication

I here remember Henry Choy:

Who guided my first tottering steps in spiritual infancy,
and taught me how to walk in Christ not by words
alone but by life example—a man totally
committed to the truth, to Christ.

And who, in the end, sealed his commitment with
his blood in some remote, unknown labor camp.
Habakkuk's commitment encapsulates
Henry's way of life:

"Though the fig tree does not bud
and there is no fruit on the vines,
though the olive crop fails
and the fields produce no food,
though there are no sheep in the pen
and no cattle in the stalls,
yet I will triumph in Yahweh;
I will rejoice in the God of my salvation!
Yahweh my Lord is my strength."

Habakkuk 3:17-19 (HCSB)

Preface

This book did not come from any plan or desire to write a book for the sake of writing a book. Rather, it grew out of an effort to address certain situations in our churches. In our churches we had non-Christians who were contemplating baptism and wanted to know how to live the Christian life. But we also had Christians who, despite having been baptized, did not know what it means to be a Christian in the biblical sense. They were living in spiritual defeat and making no headway in their "Christian" walk because they did not know what it means to follow the Lord Jesus.

These Christians come from all walks of life and every type of religious upbringing but there is a common denominator to their spiritual malaise: *a lack of commitment to God.* A Christian who is not committed to God is like a soldier who is not loyal to his own country or a family member who doesn't care about the welfare of his family. Without commitment to God, the Christian life simply does not work.

To help this situation, we set up a Bible training called *Commitment Training* (CT) which is still ongoing in our churches (Christian Disciples Church). The present book, which is based on the CT and edited for a wider audience, can be used beneficially by all churches because it deals with universal issues that confront many in the body of Christ.

CT has since been given to over a thousand people, many of whom were non-Christians seeking to be baptized. Thankfully, most of them have gone on to committing themselves to God. A minority, however, felt that the cost of discipleship is too high, and deferred making the commitment of faith.

The first CT was given in English in Hong Kong, a city in which English is not the mother tongue of most people. Hence we used a simple style of English to conduct the training. This was for clarity but also for facilitating translation, including the translation later used in the CTs given in Thailand, India, Nepal, Myanmar, and Indonesia. But even among the translators, the level of English is not necessarily high. And as for the trainees, some are not well educated even in their own languages. Here is where simplicity of language is useful, and where we see God's wisdom in having the New Testament composed in the Koine Greek of the common people as distinct from the literary Greek of the educated.

The 15 chapters in this book correspond to the 15 CT sessions, each originally an hour long. Most people can, however, read through a chapter of this book in far less time.

The thought of publishing the CT sessions was not originally in our minds. But by God's grace, many have found them helpful over the years, so the question was repeatedly asked as to why they should not be published.

The first edition of this book was published in 2001. This 2015 revised edition improves the flow of writing (e.g. by removing the repetition which is natural and effective in speech but is not needed in writing) and adds supplementary paragraphs here and there (e.g. to explain commitment in the light of biblical monotheism).

We hope that all who read this book will be inspired to commit to the one true God as we follow in the steps of His Son Jesus Christ, who lived in obedience and total commitment to his God and Father.

Eric Chang
Montreal, July 1, 2000

Bentley Chan
Montreal, October 13, 2015
biblicalmonotheism@gmail.com

PART ONE

COMMITMENT
TO GOD

Loving God with all our Heart,
Soul, Mind, and Strength

Chapter 1

Commitment in Scripture

The Christian life is not for the faint of heart because it involves tough questions that demand concrete answers rather than superficial pat answers. How do we gain eternal life? Or know that God is real? Or live as true Christians? Or die to sin? In the Bible, as we shall see, the answers to these questions are tied to our commitment to God.

As I said in the Preface, a Christian who is not committed to God is like a soldier who is not loyal to his own country or a family member who doesn't care about his family. The uncommitted Christian life simply does not work.

Commitment is not something half-hearted but is a total response to God. There is no point in discussing commitment unless we have, at the very least, the desire to commit to God. Our aim in this book is to bring about an active response to God rather than increase our head knowledge of Him. We aim for a life-changing breakthrough in our relationship with God. And for those of you who have already made some kind of commitment, my hope is that any remaining barrier that stands between you and God will be lifted. I will base this book entirely on the Bible, the word of God, and not on human opinion.

Partial commitment is worse than no commitment

Many Christians struggle in the Christian life year after year, hindered by a partial commitment to God. In most cases the problem is not zero commitment but partial commitment. But in the Bible, partial commitment is worse than no commitment. The Lord Jesus says:

> I know your works: you are neither cold nor hot. Would that you
> were either cold or hot! So, because you are lukewarm, and neither
> hot nor cold, I will spit you out of my mouth. (Rev.3:15-16, ESV)

"Cold" means turning away from God altogether. Yet in the mind of Jesus, that is not quite as bad as "lukewarm," which is neither here nor there. You may be 80 percent for God and 20 percent for the world, but the fact is that not even 95 percent is good enough for God. He requires of you nothing less than *total* commitment.

Many Christians make no progress in the Christian life because of half-hearted commitment. They don't experience the joy and peace of the Christian life and can't communicate with God because He doesn't listen to their prayers. The problem is that their commitment has not been settled: they are not totally committed to God.

We can say with absolute certainty, on the basis of God's word, that without total commitment it is impossible for you to live the Christian life. This is not a matter of theory but of reality. If you are not committed to God, you will find that your Christian life won't work. If God doesn't answer your prayers, then something needs to be sorted out in your commitment. Even among those who are serving in the full-time ministry, there are some who have commitment problems, and this is usually something they find out only after entering the ministry. It is a miserable situation to be in, for you may have given up everything in the world to serve God, only to find yourself lacking joy, spiritual power, and fellowship with God.

Where do we find commitment today?

Commitment is taught everywhere in the Bible, implicitly or explicitly. If we remove commitment from the Bible, there would be no Bible left to read, for commitment lies at the heart of our relationship with God.

When I was a young Christian in China, no one had ever told me about commitment. I did, however, have the advantage of knowing God at a time when it was dangerous to be a Christian and when our pastors were being sent to labor camps. We knew that without commitment, we would not survive as Christians. Hence commitment to God was not something that the church had to spell out explicitly.

When I later arrived in Hong Kong, I said to myself, "It's so wonderful to live in a free society where I can worship God in church and buy a Bible at a bookstore." But when I started visiting the churches in Hong Kong, I saw just how dead the Christians there were. My heart sank. I said to myself, "This is freedom? These Christians have no life in themselves!" I couldn't talk with them about the deep things of God nor even the basic things.

When I shared with them about what God had done in my life, they could not understand what I was talking about. They would give me a puzzled stare as if I had come from outer space. After hearing of my experiences of God's miracles, they would say to me, "But these things took place in the book of Acts. Did you just come out of the first century?" I said to myself, "What's happening here? I can't even fellowship with my fellow Christians."

Over time, as I listened to the sermons preached in the churches, I began to discern an indifference to the vital matter of our relationship with God. When I talked with some of the pastors, I felt I was conversing with businessmen who were more interested in church income or church property than in a deep relationship with God. They were constantly thinking of ways to expand their church facilities and raise funds to expand their organizations, much like a business trying to expand its market share. I felt sick in my heart and wondered what the problem was.

For a time I couldn't pinpoint the problem. But as I waited on God for an answer, and examined what the Bible may have to say about it, I began to see that the root problem was *a lack of commitment*. People in free societies are not interested in committing to God. The church's failure to teach commitment has resulted in the dead churches all around us. Whenever I raised the matter of commitment, many would say to me, "The cost of commitment is too high. If you teach it, no one will come to church or become a Christian." To this I would say, "But commitment is taught everywhere in the Bible."

Let us now look into the Bible to see what it says about commitment. Do not accept what I say out of any human opinion, but see for yourself what the Bible teaches about it.

Who is the God we commit to?

The Bible teaches not just commitment but *total* commitment. Commitment is the foundation of our relationship with God. It is sometimes stated explicitly in the Bible, and sometimes implicitly in verses that make sense only in connection with commitment.

We begin with an important passage from the Hebrew Bible, the Shema[1] of Deuteronomy 6:4-5:

> [4] Hear, O Israel: The LORD our God, the LORD is one. [5] You shall love the LORD your God with all your heart, with all your soul, and with all your strength.

Here total commitment to God is seen in total love for God. We are to love the LORD our God with *all* our heart, *all* our soul, *all* our strength. The triple "all" encompasses totality of devotion (all your heart), totality of person (all your soul), totality of action (all your strength).

And who is the LORD our God whom we are to love with all our heart? Here LORD is printed in small capitals, a typographical convention used in English Bibles to indicate that the original Hebrew word is YHWH or Yahweh.

Hence we are to commit to Yahweh! We are to love Yahweh our God with all our heart, all our soul, all our strength. Note the following rendering of Dt.6:4-5 in New Jerusalem Bible and how it preserves the name Yahweh:

---

[1] "Shema" (Hebrew for "hear" or "listen") is the first word of Dt.6:4 ("Hear, O Israel: The LORD our God, the LORD is one"). The Shema originally referred to the sacred proclamation of Dt.6:4 but has since been extended to include Dt.6:4-9 and 11:13-21, and Num.15:37-41. The paramount importance of the Shema is seen in the fact that it has become a Jewish confession of faith, and many Jews have died for their courageous and unwavering allegiance to it.

Listen, Israel: Yahweh our God is the one, the only Yahweh. You must love Yahweh your God with all your heart, with all your soul, with all your strength. (Dt.6:4-5, New Jerusalem Bible)

Who exactly is Yahweh?

For a discussion on who Yahweh is, see the supplementary note at the end of this chapter. Here is a summary in seven points:

- "Yahweh" is God's personal name
- "Yahweh" is the primary term for God in the Hebrew Bible
- "Yahweh" is a unique name that never refers to false gods
- Yahweh is the one and only God
- Yahweh is the sole Creator of the universe
- Yahweh is the God of Abraham, Isaac, and Jacob
- Yahweh is the God and Father of Jesus Christ

Loving God with our whole being

Having looked at Deuteronomy 6:4-5, we now extend this to include verses 6 and 7, in order to see the degree of our commitment to God:

Hear, O Israel: The LORD our God, the LORD is one. You shall love the LORD your God with all your heart and with all your soul and with all your might. And these words that I command you today shall be on your heart. You shall teach them diligently to your children, and shall talk of them when you sit in your house, and when you walk by the way, and when you lie down, and when you rise. (Dt.6:4-7, ESV)

Whether you are asleep or awake, sitting or walking, inside or outside the house, you must love the LORD your God with all your heart, with all your soul, with all your strength. This is total love and total commitment, and is repeated in Deuteronomy 11:13:

> If you faithfully obey the commands I am giving you today—to love
> the LORD your God and to serve him with all your heart and with
> all your soul ... (NIV)

This is reaffirmed by the Lord Jesus in Matthew 22:37:

> And Jesus said to him, "You shall love the Lord your God with all
> your heart and with all your soul and with all your mind."

Hence, in both the Old and New Testaments, total commitment is
seen in loving the LORD our God (Yahweh) with our whole being.

Is the word "commit" really in the Bible?

Is the word *commit* or *commitment* found in the Bible or are we just
making it up? Before answering the question, we note that the absence
of a word in the Bible does not necessarily mean it is biblically incor-
rect. Some biblical concepts are conveyed by words not found in the
Bible. An example is the word *sacrament* which refers to baptism and
the Lord's Supper.

Another example is *atonement*, a word that refers to something
achieved by Christ's death: he died to atone for—to pay for—our sins
in order to reconcile us to God. The word occurs only once in the New
Testament of KJV, in Romans 5:11, a verse in which modern Bibles are
more likely to use *reconciliation*. But whether *atonement* is used or not,
it expresses the truth of what was accomplished for us at the cross.

But *commit* does not fall into the same category as *sacrament* or
atonement because *commit* is a word that is actually used many times
in the Bible in relation to God. It is found, for example, in Psalm 31:5
of most Bibles: "Into your hands I commit my spirit; redeem me, O
Yahweh, the God of truth". When Jesus was dying on the cross, he
said, "Father, into your hands I commit my spirit" (Lk.23:46). To commit one's spirit to God is to entrust oneself totally to Him.

"Commit" is found in Psalm 37:5 of most Bibles: "Commit your
way to the LORD; trust in him, and he will act". Again the basic idea is
to entrust, to put something into someone's care. To commit my spirit
to God is to put my life, my spirit, into God's care.

Proverbs 16:3 says, "Commit what you do to the LORD, and your plans will be established". Entrust your work and endeavors to God so that He may cause them to bear fruit according to His will.

Hence *commit* does not belong to the class of words such as *sacrament* or *atonement* in terms of its presence or absence in the Bible. On the contrary, *commit* is used many times in the Bible in relation to God.

"Therefore let those who suffer according to the will of God commit their souls to Him in doing good, as to a faithful Creator" (1Pet.4:19, NKJV). The Greek word for *soul* also means life. To save your soul is to save your life; to lose your soul is to lose your life. To commit your soul to God is to commit your life to God.

This is in fact the biblical principle of faith: entrusting yourself to God. Faith is not just believing in certain doctrines but committing yourself to God. Believing with all your heart that an elevator can take you up is fundamentally different from your stepping into it. If you don't step into the elevator, you won't go up even if you believe with all your heart that it can take you up. You have to walk into the elevator and entrust yourself to it. In the Bible, to entrust is to trust "into". When you entrust yourself to the elevator, you step *into* the elevator and let it carry you up.

Likewise you are not saved merely by believing that God can save you. Satan also believes that God has a plan of salvation but that won't save him. The demons believe that God is one, yet they tremble (James 2:19). To be saved, you must believe in God in such a way as to commit or entrust yourself to Him.

In most Bibles, *entrust* is the word used in 1Pet.4:19 (quoted) and in verses such as 1Tim.1:18 and 2Tim.1:12 and 2:2. Jesus committed himself to God his Father, entrusting his spirit to Him, when he suffered and died for us:

> When they hurled their insults at him, he did not retaliate; when he suffered, he made no threats. Instead, he entrusted himself to him who judges justly. (1Pet.2:23, NIV)

The story of a former gangster

We now move from the explicit to the implicit use of "commit". The first words Jesus preached at the start of his ministry after his baptism were: "Repent, for the kingdom of heaven is near" (Mt.4:17).

Here the Greek word for "repent" means a change of heart, a change of the mind, a change of attitude. To repent is to turn your life around. You were heading in one direction, now you do a U-turn.

But is repentance even possible without commitment? This is what I mean by "implied" commitment. The word "commitment" might not be stated explicitly, yet without commitment, there can be no change or repentance. We are not talking of mere superficial reform but a far-reaching transformation from one state of the heart to another.

I heard the testimony of a former Chicago gangster who shared on what it meant for him to repent and become a Christian. Leaving his gangster way of life would, in the first place, put him in constant danger of being killed. His former gang wanted him dead because he knew too many of its secrets. He could walk into any police station and give the names of the gangsters right up to the boss.

Secondly, because he had acquired money and property by crime, repentance meant giving everything back to his victims.

It turns out that repentance is not so trivial after all. Could this former gangster have repented the way he did without commitment? He put his life on the line. He sold everything he had and tried to give back every penny until he had nothing left.

For most of us, becoming a Christian is not quite so dramatic. But no matter what may be our circumstances, we still have to change in our own ways. In every case of repentance, commitment is needed because without it, change would not be possible.

If we are unwilling to commit to God, we shouldn't be talking about repentance or else we will make it a hollow term. We often think of repentance in terms of feeling sorry for one's sins but that is not the biblical meaning of repentance. True repentance involves a fundamental change in heart and mind, not just feeling sorry. The former gangster was more than sorry when he put his life on the line; in fact the gang did try to kill him once. He sold everything he had and became penniless. Becoming a Christian cost him everything; it was a change that took total commitment.

Commitment and the kingdom of God

We now proceed to the kingdom of God, a central theme of the New Testament and Jesus' teaching. Can you proclaim the kingdom of God without speaking of, or at least implying, commitment? You cannot do this except by ignoring the biblical meaning of "kingdom". But if you understand what is commitment, you will know what is the kingdom of God. If you take commitment out of the kingdom, you will be left with a hollow term that has been emptied of its meaning.

The kingdom of God fundamentally means *the kingship of God*. It declares God as King. The traditional word *kingdom*, which has become standard in our Bibles, may confuse us in this modern age because we would understand it in terms of territory as in "the United Kingdom". But that is not the fundamental meaning of *kingdom* in the New Testament. The kingdom of God fundamentally means the kingship of God—His reign, His rule, His government—and is not primarily concerned with territory (see chapter 11 of the present book, 2nd footnote, on the meaning of the Greek word *basileia*). But because *kingdom* is used in the King James Bible, it has become a standard term, though a few modern translations are starting to use *kingship*.

The kingship of God simply means that God is king in your life. If you think about what it means in practice, you will see that it involves total commitment. Without commitment, you cannot move from a self-centered way of life to a life in which God is king. In the old way of life, you did as you wished and sinned as you wished. You did selfish things and lost your temper as you wished. But now that you live under God's kingship, you no longer do what you used to do. You even have to get God's permission to get angry!

"I am angry. May I lose my temper?"
"No."
"What can I do? I am about to explode."

Just quiet down and depend on God's help to contain your anger. It doesn't mean that a Christian may never be angry, but it does mean that you don't lose your temper and go out of control, smashing chairs and throwing dishes. You may be angry but you don't behave in a way that dishonors God.

Anger is not necessarily wrong. Paul says, "Be angry and do not sin" (Eph.4:26). Anger may be justified when we see evil or injustice, but we must not behave in a way that dishonors God. This requires a lot of self-control, a quality which is of the fruit of the Spirit (Gal.5:22-23).

Is it possible to submit to God's kingship without commitment? Not even remotely. Living under God's kingship takes commitment: "I entrust myself to you and submit to your kingship in response to your love for me." But God won't force you to submit to His kingship, for it is something of your own free choice.

Are we making God a constitutional monarch?

For most people the kingship of God is a vague concept. God is treated as a constitutional monarch in the way the Queen of England is a constitutional monarch—a monarch in name. She is honored as Queen and is addressed "Your Majesty" but she has no true governing power. It is the Prime Minister who holds the real authority. The word *majesty* originally meant supreme power, yet in a constitutional monarchy, the one who is addressed "Your Majesty" holds no real power.

A similar situation is seen in the lives of many Christians. You might address God as Lord and King, but you do your own thing. You are the Prime Minister who holds the real power whereas God is only a constitutional monarch who exercises no control over your life. You are a Christian in name, without true commitment to God.

England is nominally a monarchy yet also a democracy. Technically, a democracy cannot be a monarchy for that would be an oxymoron, for either the king rules or the people rule. But today we have worked out an arrangement in which the king or queen retains the title of monarch but doesn't hold real power. It is the elected representative, the Prime Minister, who holds the real governing power. He and his government write the agenda for Parliament and the Queen duly gives her assent.

In the Christian life, we likewise decide what we will do. We present our agenda to God whom we call Lord and King, yet in effect we are saying to Him, "Please sign on the dotted line and bless me." We may have the courtesy to say "please" but if God doesn't bless us, the offering will go down next week. We were planning to give $50 but now we give $5 because God didn't bless us the way we wanted.

But God's kingship doesn't work like that. If you make Him the constitutional monarch of your life, you will end up the loser. You may fool yourself but you won't fool God. Your life will be an empty palace in which you do your own thing but God is not there.

Commitment and the Sermon on the Mount

The Sermon on the Mount (in Matthew 5, 6, 7) is crucial to a correct understanding of Jesus' teaching, yet we cannot even understand the Sermon itself because we have mentally subtracted commitment from it.

When you look at the Beatitudes (the "blessed" statements in Mt.5:3-12), would you say that those described as "blessed" would be regarded as blessed by the standards of the world? Blessed are the poor, yet the world thinks the rich are blessed. Blessed are those who mourn and weep, yet the world expects joy and laughter from those who are blessed. Blessed are the meek, yet the world admires the dominant and the assertive. The Beatitudes conclude with, "Blessed are those who have been persecuted for the sake of righteousness". Since when is persecution a blessing? If you are persecuted for being a Christian, would you feel it is a blessing?

What the Bible describes as a blessing, the world doesn't consider to be a blessing. Here we see that God's values are the opposite of man's:

> "For my thoughts are not your thoughts, neither are your ways my ways," declares Yahweh. "As the heavens are higher than the earth, so are my ways higher than your ways and my thoughts than your thoughts." (Isaiah 55:8-9)

I have always said that the Bible could not have been invented by man, for it is so different from the way we think.

Commitment and grace

Commitment is inseparable from grace, for without commitment we cannot avail of God's grace and power, whether it is the power to understand His word or to fulfill His commands. Sooner or later you will find yourself in a situation in which you say, "Lord, this is imposs- ible to fulfill, but because you command it, I will do it by your grace." With this kind of commitment, you will experience God's power.

After we fulfill the Beatitudes, the next step is to fulfill the verses that come after the Beatitudes: Matthew 5:13, "You are the salt of the earth," and verse 14, "You are the light of the world." These phrases sound familiar to us, yet the church is all too often not the salt of the earth or the light of the world. Again the root problem is a lack of commitment. You cannot bypass the Beatitudes and proceed to verses 13 and 14. If you try to skip over the Beatitudes to become the salt of the earth, it won't work. You become the salt of the earth only when you are committed to fulfilling the Beatitudes: to be poor in spirit, to mourn for sin, to be persecuted for the sake of righteousness.

Many Christians have not experienced God's transforming power. But if we let God change us, we will experience His power and know Him as the living God. We will then move from darkness to light: "You were once darkness but now you are light in the Lord. Live as children of light" (Eph.5:8).

The determination not to sin

The Lord Jesus continues in the Sermon on the Mount:

> If your right eye causes you to sin, gouge it out and throw it away. It is better for you to lose one part of your body than for your whole body to be thrown into hell. And if your right hand causes you to sin, cut it off and throw it away. It is better for you to lose one part of your body than for your whole body to go into hell. (Mt.5:29-30)

This is true commitment! In fact the word "commitment" may be too weak to describe this decisive and frightening course of action. You must be willing to cut off your right hand if it causes you to sin. Without this kind of commitment, Jesus warns, you could end up in hell.

But Jesus is not so superficial as to mean that you can deal with the problem of sin merely by cutting off your hand. We might as well chop off our heads for our brains would still be sinning after our hand has been cut off. In the previous verse (Mt.5:28), Jesus says that the problem of sin lies in the "heart". He then uses vivid language to describe the kind of commitment that is needed to fight sin. He doesn't mean that you literally cut off your hand but that you must have the determination and commitment to do whatever it takes not to sin. It is better to lose something such as your hand or eye than to end up in hell.

Our God is a loving God yet also a holy God. Holiness is a central teaching in the Bible yet it is seldom taught in the churches today. Commitment to God cannot be separated from commitment to holiness.

Discerning the truth

Finally, how do we know if a teaching is true or false? Jesus says, "If anyone's will is to do God's will, he will know whether the teaching is from God or whether I am speaking on my own authority." (Jn.7:17) Again we see the call to commitment. If you are committed to doing God's will, you will know whether a teaching is true or false, whether it is from God or from man.

I have absolute confidence in God's truth because ever since I have come to know Him many years ago, I have put this verse into practice. I testify it is true. I have staked my life on it, and I know it is true. If you are willing to commit to God, you will experience Him as the living God!

Supplementary Note

Who is Yahweh?

In English Bibles, when the word "Lord" is printed in small capitals as LORD, it indicates that the original word in the Hebrew text is YHWH or Yahweh. For example, the familiar phrase "the word of the LORD" is in Hebrew literally "the word of Yahweh" (e.g. 1 Kings 18:1, "the word of Yahweh came to Elijah"). In Psalm 23:1, "The LORD is my shepherd" is literally "Yahweh is my shepherd". The familiar term, "the Spirit of the LORD," is literally "the Spirit of Yahweh" (e.g. Ezekiel 11:5, "the Spirit of Yahweh fell upon me").

In fact the standard translation of Isaiah 42:8 makes no sense ("I am the LORD, that is my name") unless the name Yahweh is restored, as in NJB and HCSB: "I am Yahweh, that is my name".

The typographical convention of rendering "Lord" as LORD in small capitals is explained in the prefaces of most modern Bibles. For example, ESV says, "The ESV usually renders the personal name of God (YHWH) with the word LORD (printed in small capitals)."

We now make seven brief observations about Yahweh, with emphasis on the identity of Yahweh. Who is Yahweh?

1. "Yahweh" is God's personal name

We have just quoted ESV as saying that YHWH is the "personal name of God". This crucial fact, that "Yahweh" is God's personal name, is seen throughout the Hebrew Bible, for example, in the Ten Commandments: "You shall not take the name of Yahweh your God in vain" (Ex.20:7). It is seen also in Exodus 3:15, where God said to Moses:

> Say this to the people of Israel, "Yahweh, the God of your fathers, the God of Abraham, the God of Isaac, and the God of Jacob, has sent me to you." *This is my name forever,* and thus I am to be remembered throughout all generations. (ESV, with "Yahweh" in the original Hebrew text restored)

When God said, "This is my name forever" (see the italics), He was referring to His own name Yahweh which is mentioned in the same verse. The word "forever" indicates that Yahweh is to be God's name not just for one generation but for all eternity; indeed it is "to be remembered throughout all generations".

It is standard knowledge among Bible scholars that Yahweh is God's personal name, as seen in Bible encyclopedias such as ISBE ("Yahweh is the only truly personal name of God in Israel's faith"), in Hebrew dictionaries such as TWOT ("Yahweh, the personal name of God"), and in Bible commentaries such as UBC ("the knowledge of the personal name of God, Yahweh, was arguably the greatest gift of God entrusted to Israel").[2]

In fact some Bible scholars are calling for a return to the original name Yahweh. A standard theological dictionary says:

> The "translation" LORD is something of a problem from various perspectives. LORD obscures the fact that Yahweh is a name and not a title ... In view of this reality, it could be argued that, as with other personal names, *we simply transliterate what the original Hebrew was thought to be—Yahweh.*[3] (italics added)

2. "Yahweh" is the primary term for God in the Hebrew Bible

Whereas "Yahweh" occurs 6,828 times in the Hebrew Bible, "Elohim" (God, god) occurs about 2,600 times. Hence the primary term for God in the Hebrew Bible (the Old Testament) is not "God" but "Yahweh".

3. "Yahweh" is a unique name that never refers to false gods

Most of the 2,600 or so instances of "Elohim" (God) refer to the God of Israel; yet over 200 times it refers to false gods such as the golden calf (Ex.32:4) and the goddess Ashtoreth (1Ki.11:33). By contrast, the name

---

[2] ISBE (*God, Names of*); TWOT (484a, YHWH); *Understanding the Bible Commentary* (Dt.5:11).

[3] *New International Dictionary of Old Testament Theology* (vol.5, *Yahweh*).

"Yahweh" always refers to the God of Israel and never to false gods, *without exception.*

4. Yahweh is the one and only God

Yahweh says, "I am Yahweh, and there is no other, besides me there is no God" (Isaiah 45:5), and "there is no other god besides me" (v.21).

5. Yahweh is the only Creator of the universe

Yahweh says, "I am Yahweh, who made all things, who alone stretched out the heavens, who spread out the earth by myself." (Isaiah 44:24)

6. Yahweh is the God of Abraham, Isaac, and Jacob

Yahweh God instructed Moses to tell the Israelites: "Yahweh, the God of your fathers, the God of Abraham, the God of Isaac, and the God of Jacob, has sent me to you." (Exodus 3:15)

7. Yahweh is the God and Father of Jesus Christ

As a preliminary point, we note that Yahweh is our Father: "Is this the way you repay Yahweh, you foolish and unwise people? Is he not your Father who created you?" (Dt.32:6; cf. Mal.2:10). But more specifically, Yahweh is also the God and Father of Jesus Christ: "I am ascending to my Father and your Father, to my God and your God" (Jn.20:17). In John 17:3, Jesus addresses his Father as "the only true God," an identification that agrees with Isaiah 45:5: "I am Yahweh, and there is no other, besides me there is no God".

Chapter 2

Commitment is from the Heart

Commitment of the heart

In this chapter we show that commitment runs through the Sermon on the Mount. Let us start with the following statement by the Lord Jesus:

> It was also said, "Whoever divorces his wife, let him give her a certificate of divorce." But I say to you that everyone who divorces his wife, except on the ground of sexual immorality, makes her commit adultery, and whoever marries a divorced woman commits adultery. (Mt.5:31-32, ESV)

What has this to do with commitment? In a marriage, two persons commit to each other. When the commitment breaks down at the heart level, divorce is often the next step. Where there is no heart commitment, marriage loses its God-intended meaning. Some people marry for money or citizenship, or by the compulsion of circumstance. But regardless of the reason, can there be a meaningful marriage without commitment?

Sin is fundamentally non-commitment or contra-commitment; it is the refusal to be committed to a person or to God. That is why adultery harms the marriage commitment, and why God says, "I hate divorce"

(Mal.2:16). God hates non-commitment in a marriage just as He hates non-commitment to Him by His people.

In the Garden of Eden, God told Adam not to eat the fruit of a particular tree, yet the whole event is summed up in Adam's disobedience. Can there be true obedience without commitment? "Obedience" is another word that has no more meaning when commitment is removed from it, for what will remain is no longer heart obedience.

Commitment in speech

In the Sermon on the Mount, Jesus talks about divorce one moment, then trustworthiness of speech the next moment. His statements in the Sermon may seem disconnected until we see that they all bring out different aspects of commitment.

> Again you have heard that it was said to those of old, "You shall not swear falsely, but shall perform to the Lord what you have sworn." But I say to you, Do not take an oath at all, either by heaven, for it is the throne of God, or by the earth, for it is his footstool, or by Jerusalem, for it is the city of the great King. And do not take an oath by your head, for you cannot make one hair white or black. Let what you say be simply "Yes" or "No"; anything more than this comes from evil. (Mt.5:33-37, ESV)

If I say *yes*, I commit myself to doing what I said I will do. If I say *no*, I refrain from doing what I said I won't do. Either way there is commitment. Your character has to manifest commitment in your speech whether it is "yes" or "no," with nothing more said. No vow is needed. Making a vow adds nothing to what you have said. A vow is often said for the purpose of convincing someone that you mean what you have said. But fundamentally, your character has to be such that you always mean what you say, vow or no vow.

As we go through the Sermon on the Mount, we will see its underlying theme of commitment. As for vows, there is such a transformation of character that our word becomes our bond and commitment. You wouldn't trust someone who could one moment say "yes" and the next moment say "no." And because God's own character expresses commitment, He cannot tolerate the non-commitment which is so typical of the unregenerate person.

Love is ultimately a commitment

Continuing in the Sermon on the Mount, the Lord Jesus says:

> You have heard that it was said, "You shall love your neighbor and hate your enemy." But I say to you, Love your enemies and pray for those who persecute you, so that you may be sons of your Father who is in heaven. For he makes his sun rise on the evil and on the good, and sends rain on the just and on the unjust. For if you love those who love you, what reward do you have? Do not even the tax collectors do the same? And if you greet only your brothers, what more are you doing than others? Do not even the Gentiles do the same? You therefore must be perfect, as your heavenly Father is perfect. (Mt.5:43-48, ESV)

The opening statement is, "You shall love your neighbor". Ponder for a moment on the meaning of love. Fundamentally, what is love if there is no commitment? Can you give me a definition of love that excludes commitment? That would be impossible because commitment is the essence of love. Many people miss this vital point and think of love as a feeling. But the biblical meaning of love is a love that is rooted in commitment rather than feelings.

Over the years I have asked people who were planning on getting married, "What do you like about him?" or "What do you like about her?" To my surprise, often the answer is, "I like his/her looks". And what does that mean? Do you like the hairstyle? Or the eyes? I would scratch my head and say to myself, "Are beautiful eyes going to be the foundation of this marriage?" Sometimes they go deeper: "I like his/her style." Again, what does that mean? Are you referring to the way one talks or dresses? If you fall in love for superficial reasons, what will happen when he or she falls sick, grows old, or has thin hair? Is that the end of the relationship?

Surely we have to build commitment on a firmer foundation. At the very least I won't commit myself in marriage unless the two of us share the same life goals. We will travel the same road, fight the same battles, and strive for the same goals. This will provide a stronger basis for committing to each another.

A marriage based on feelings or external attractiveness but not deep substance has no foundation for commitment. If you take commitment out of love, the word *love* will have no more meaning as far as its biblical definition is concerned.

Three points on love and commitment

1. Love is based on commitment, not emotions
We love the neighbor or love one another, not because you are lovely or I am lovely, but because God is lovely and has commanded us to love. This eliminates emotions as the foundation of love. Commitment is the only sure basis on which love between people can survive. If you base a commitment on "liking" the other person, the commitment will not survive, for it takes only one careless word to wreck the relationship. If we take commitment out of love, there would be no more love to talk about.

2. The commitment to love is a matter of obedience
The motivation of love should not be mere liking. In Jesus' teaching, the reason we love and commit is not that the other person is lovely but that God has commanded us to love. Hence the commitment to love is an act of obedience.

We love the unlovely because God, who is lovely, has commanded us to love the unlovely, even our enemy. From your perspective, your enemy is the most unlovely of all. If you love only the lovely, it would be impossible for you to love the enemy. It is hard enough to love a friend when you know his or her shortcomings, never mind loving an enemy.

The fact is that we cannot love our enemy except by God's power. We have enough difficulty loving our friends. Many wives have a hard time loving their husbands, and many husbands their wives. But where there is commitment on our part, there is grace from God that empowers us to do what we normally cannot do. When you live by the power of God, you will know that He is real.

I know that God is real because I have taken up the challenge to commit to Him and, contrary to my nature, to do His will. When I do what I normally cannot do, I know that His grace is empowering me. Many Christians find no joy in the Christian life because they haven't taken up the challenge of commitment. But if you take up this challenge, you will experience God's power.

3. Commitment comes from a heart transformed by God's power

True commitment comes from the heart and is not an external performance for others to see. This comes out in Matthew 6 in the Sermon on the Mount with its teaching on fasting, prayer, and almsgiving. Commitment comes from a transformed nature, not by gritting one's teeth and saying, "I will see this through." What we might call "heroic commitment" is really nothing more than an attempt to do God's will in our own strength. It is sure to fail because sooner or later we will get exhausted and frustrated. You may be sincere in your commitment but you are still depending on your own strength. You need to commit to God from your heart and draw strength from Him.

The commitment that Jesus calls for in the Sermon on the Mount is impossible except by God's power. I have seen Christians make an effort at commitment and then give up because they are doing it in their own strength. Try loving your enemy in your own strength, and you won't make it beyond a minute or two.

The other side of the picture: God's commitment to us

Let us delve deeper into commitment, right into God's very nature. In First John chapter 4, twice we see the monumental statement that *God is love*:

> The one who does not love does not know God, because God is love (v.8) .... God is love, and the one who remains in love remains in God, and God remains in him. (v.16)

Twice it is said that God is love. Since God is love, those who follow Him must also walk in love. And since commitment is the foundation of love, commitment is intrinsic to the nature of God who is love.

But our commitment to God is incomplete until we see the other side of the picture: God's commitment to us. This is seen in the same chapter: "We love because He first loved us" (1Jn.4:19). Similarly, we commit to God because He first committed to us.

In the remainder of the present chapter, we will look at God's commitment to us rather than our commitment to God. Indeed, towards the end of Matthew 5, the Sermon on the Mount shifts its focus from our commitment to God to God's commitment to us. Jesus says:

> … that you may be sons of your Father in heaven. He causes his sun to rise on the evil and the good, and sends rain on the righteous and the unrighteous. (Mt.5:45, NIV)

Here we see God's commitment to us on the basis of the fact that we are His creatures. When He sends rain on the earth, does He bless only the righteous, steering the rain to their fields while the unrighteous receive no rain and starve? The biblical answer is that God shows His basic commitment to all people whether they are righteous or unrighteous. He gives rain and sunshine to the unrighteous even if they don't thank Him for a successful harvest but attribute it to their own industriousness. But if God holds back the rain for a year, they will begin to see their human limitations. If the rain is held back two years, their helplessness will become acute. If God holds back the rain for three years as in the days of Elijah when God punished the people of Israel for their disobedience, their situation will become unimaginably dire.

God is committed to His creatures. Whether you are righteous or unrighteous, God gives you rain, sunshine, air to breathe, and health. In this world do we see a pattern of good health among the righteous and poor health among the unrighteous? In fact, if there is any pattern at all, it may be the other way around, in which case you might feel that God is partial towards the unrighteous. Psalm 73 laments that the wicked prosper while the righteous suffer.

God our Creator is committed to His creatures even if they don't thank Him. Do you thank God for what He has given you? Are you committed to your Creator? Many people are not committed, not even when they have good health or a high-paying job. Isn't it amazing that God is gracious to a world that doesn't acknowledge Him? But there is more:

> Look at the birds of the air; they do not sow or reap or store away in barns, and yet your heavenly Father feeds them. Are you not much more valuable than they? …. And why do you worry about clothes? See how the lilies of the field grow. They do not labor or spin. (Mt.6:26,28, NIV)

Look around you. Do birds depend on things such as barns and tractors? They don't even sow seeds! Yet they are vibrant creatures that fly and hop and sing. God has seen to it that His creatures have food and other provisions.

Look at the flowers around you. One thing I like about Hong Kong is that there are flowers all year round. I wonder if the people of Hong Kong might take flowers for granted. In Canada, flowers bloom only at a certain time of the year, but when they bloom, I would often pause and admire their beauty. Not even Solomon in his kingly glory could compete with the beauty of flowers (v.29).

When you bring home a rose, you admire its beauty, but it dies in a few days' time. But while it was living, it had value and meaning in displaying God's beautiful design in creation and His care in providing for the needs of His creation. If God clothes the grass of the field with beauty, which is alive today and gone tomorrow, will He not do much more for you, "O men of little faith" (v.30)?

Trusting God for our needs

Jesus is saying all this not to increase our theological knowledge of God's attributes, but to teach us to trust God for our physical needs. In China I lived by the words in Matthew 6 every day for three years. Each morning when I got up with no food for the day, I would say, "Father, you look after the birds of the air. I have nothing to eat today,

so please look after me, your child." Every day my Father would provide for me without fail. You can imagine what that does to your faith
as it is being built on the solid experience of trusting Him, committing
to Him, and knowing that His word never fails. I know the truth of
these words, and I hope you do too. It would be a great pity if the only
thing you know in this world is securing your own life with your own
hands, at the cost of not experiencing God's reality.

At the conclusion of the first full-time discipleship training which I
led in Montreal, I told the trainees that they will be sent to the province
of Ontario. I said to them, "You're going to learn to trust in God. I'm
sending you out to Ontario with only a few dollars in your pockets,
and for the next month you're going to trust God for all your needs."
They had only enough money to travel to Ontario, plus a few dollars
for the month ahead. I said, "We will see whether God looks after His
servants or not, whether He will provide for your needs or not. If the
Bible is not true or God is not real, forget about committing your life
to serving Him. What's the point of giving up your careers to serve a
God you can't put your trust in? If you end up starving in the coming
month, forget the whole matter, and pack your bags and go home."

When they returned to Montreal a month later, they weren't any
thinner than when they began their journey. They were rejoicing in
God and sharing how He had provided for their needs for a whole
month. One month isn't a long time, but even in that short time they
had learned a lot about God's reality. I know that my God is real!

This is not tempting God but applying what Jesus has taught us in
places like Luke 12. Trust God to meet your needs. Don't be anxious
about food and clothing. Don't store up treasure on earth but give your
riches to the poor. Then go out in full dependence on God and see
what He will do. That is commitment! What's the point of talking
about commitment without getting real about it? And how did the disciples follow the Lord Jesus? They lived as he lived. Just as Jesus had
nowhere to lay his head, so they received no adequate financial support
from any earthly source. Every day they would venture forth, trusting
in the Father.

Do you dare entrust your life to God? If you don't consider Him
trustworthy enough to look after you in this life, what is the basis of

your confidence of having eternal life in the age to come? You may be hoping for the best, yet you aren't really sure that after you die, God will raise you up. If you can't trust in Him now, how will you trust in Him for your future? That is why many Christians lack conviction in their Christian message or life direction. They have not understood God's commitment to them. It is most exciting to live in this world when you know that the eternal God is committed to you! This will bring peace and joy into your life in a way that few have experienced.

Jesus tells us not to be anxious over things such as clothing (Mt. 6:28). Anxiety is the negation, even denial, of commitment. But when I am committed, I am confident. I am no longer anxious but have peace in my heart. When I know that God is committed to me, I have nothing to be anxious about.

God's further commitment to us, His children

Matthew 7 takes us to the heart of the Sermon on the Mount, right into God's commitment to us. We have seen that His commitment to us is based on the fact of creation, for we are His creatures. But beyond that basic commitment, He is committed to His children on a deeper level:

> Ask, and it will be given to you; seek, and you will find; knock, and it will be opened to you. For everyone who asks receives, and the one who seeks finds, and to the one who knocks it will be opened. Or which one of you, if his son asks him for bread, will give him a stone? Or if he asks for a fish, will give him a serpent? If you then, who are evil, know how to give good gifts to your children, how much more will your Father who is in heaven give good things to those who ask him! (Mt.7:7-11, ESV)

If God is your Father, how much more than your earthly father will He give good gifts to you! He will see to it that your needs are met. In China, when I was by myself and penniless, with no place to sleep, I had to depend on God totally. Every morning I would say, "Lord, I am your child and you are my Father," and He would never fail me.

God the Creator is committed to us His creatures, which is why even the unbeliever will have his needs met. But if further we are God's children, He will be committed to us on a yet deeper level, as Father to son or daughter. "But to all who have received him, who believed in his name, he gave the right to become children of God." (Jn.1:12)

In summary, God's commitment to us is expressed on two levels: the level of creation, expressed to all mankind; and the level of sonship, expressed to His children. If we are the sons of God, we will experience His commitment on these two levels. Let it sink into your heart that God is committed to you!

How God expresses His commitment to us depends on how we commit to Him

A vital principle emerges from the Sermon on the Mount: God is committed to us, but how He expresses His commitment depends on how we express our commitment to Him. Whether He blesses us or judges us, whether He deals with us graciously or sternly, depends on how we respond to Him. Even God's judgment is an expression of His commitment to us.

Different people experience God differently because they commit to Him differently. You will experience God in one manner or another, depending on your commitment to Him. If you are committed to God, He will respond to you in one way. If you are not committed to God, He will respond in a different way. Matthew 6:1 says:

> Beware of practicing your righteousness before other people in order to be seen by them, for then you will have no reward from your Father who is in heaven. (ESV)

If you practice your righteousness for others to see, you won't get a reward from God. But if you practice your righteousness in secret (e.g. by giving to the poor in secret), "your Father who sees in secret will reward you" (v.4). In the one case you get no reward from God; in the other you get a reward. How you respond to God and His word will determine whether you get a reward or not. God's commitment to you is always there, but how you experience it depends on how you respond to Him.

The same principle is repeated in verse 5 (no reward from God) and verse 6 (reward from God), and again in verse 16 (no reward from God) and verse 18 (reward from God). Those who receive reward from men in the form of human praise won't get any further reward from God.

The link between God's commitment and our commitment continues in the Sermon on the Mount. Whether we are forgiven depends on whether we forgive others. God shows His commitment to us by forgiving us if we forgive, or not forgiving us if we don't forgive:

> If you forgive men when they sin against you, your heavenly Father will also forgive you. But if you do not forgive men their sins, your Father will not forgive your sins. (Mt.6:14-15, NIV)

Matthew 7:1-2 brings out a similar principle:

> Do not judge or you too will be judged. For in the same way you judge others, you will be judged, and with the measure you use, it will be measured to you. (NIV)

If you are committed to someone, you will do what is good for him or her. But judging a person is an act that elevates you above commitment: You are saying that you don't owe him any commitment, yet you stand above him as judge. You have taken God's place in regard to that person, but without God's love and commitment. Jesus says that the standard you measure to others will be measured to you. Exegetically this is a "divine passive," an indirect reference to God: God is not mentioned explicitly but it is implied that He is the one who will treat you according to how you treat others. It also reveals whether you are obeying God. If you judge others, you are disobeying God's command not to judge. If you love others, you are obeying His command to love. If you judge others, God will judge you. If you love others, God will pour forth His love on you.

To experience God's abundant love, simply obey the command to love. To experience God's judgment (which is also an expression of His commitment to us), go out and judge others; then you will see what God will do to you even though you are a Christian.

The same principle is at work in Matthew 7:7: "Ask and it will be given to you; seek and you will find; knock and it will be opened to you." Again it is your act that draws out a response from God. Ask and it will be given to you. If you don't ask, you won't get anything. If you seek after God with all your heart, you will find Him. If you don't seek after God, you won't find Him. If you don't knock on the door of the Kingdom, it won't be opened to you.

The Christian life is not one in which we sit back and wait for something to drop out of the sky and onto our laps. It involves a dynamic of asking, seeking, and knocking. God will respond to our actions because He doesn't want us to be puppets but people who take the initiative to seek what is good in His eyes. The Christian life is one of constant interaction between God and us. Jesus continues:

> Likewise every good tree bears good fruit, but a bad tree bears bad fruit. A good tree cannot bear bad fruit, and a bad tree cannot bear good fruit. Every tree that does not bear good fruit is cut down and thrown into the fire. (Mt.7:17-19, NIV)

If we bear good fruit, we will receive blessing from God. If we bear bad fruit, His commitment to us will be expressed in judgment, for every bad tree will be cut down and thrown into the fire of God's judgment. Never take God's judgment to be non-commitment on God's part. In fact, judgment is an act of God's absolute commitment to His creatures. The responsibility of committing to God rests on us. The buck is in our hands, and we cannot pass it back to God.

Not just in the New Testament but also the Old Testament do we see the principle that God's response is based on our response:

> The LORD has rewarded me according to my righteousness, according to the cleanness of my hands in his sight. To the faithful you show yourself faithful, to the blameless you show yourself blameless, to the pure you show yourself pure, but to the crooked you show yourself shrewd. (Psalm 18:24-26, NIV)

The pure will find God pure, the loyal will find God loyal, the crooked will find God hard to deal with. God is to you what you are to Him. If you start playing games with God, you will end up in a losing game. If you are honest with God, He will be honest with you. God is never dishonest but if you have a dishonest or crooked mind, your view of God as a dishonest God will be shaped by your negative experience of Him. Different people experience God differently. Some don't experience Him at all because they don't respond to Him.

A psalmist wrote, "Surely you will reward each person according to what he has done" (Ps.62:12), for God responds to us according to what we do. The same principle applies to Israel: "I will deal with them according to their own conduct, and I will judge them by their own standards. Then they will know that I am the LORD." (Eze.7:27, HCSB)

The way my daughter relates to me affects the way I relate to her. If she is disobedient, she may discover that her dad can be severe. But if she is obedient, she will discover that her dad is very kind. I am puzzled as to why she would sometimes choose to draw severity from me when I am more than happy to show her kindness. If you are a parent, you would know this very well. God likewise wants to bless us instead of being hard on us. So why would we want to get into trouble with Him? As we saw in Matthew 7:11, God is willing to pour His blessings on you, so why not give Him a chance to do that for you?

Choose God's blessing

In Deuteronomy 27 and 28, God set before Israel the choice between curses (chapter 27) and blessings (chapter 28). He doesn't want to curse us, but if we live in sin and evil, His commitment to us will be expressed in judgment.

Mounts Ebal and Gerizim are the two mountains in Samaria where Deuteronomy 27 and 28 took place. The curses were pronounced from Ebal, the blessings from Gerizim. It was an impressive event in which all Israel was gathered in the open, and they heard the curses and the blessings being called out from the respective mountains. Whenever I travel to Israel and pass between the two mountains, I would remember this event. Whether we receive a blessing or a curse is something of our own choice, a principle that runs through the Old and New Testaments. God said to Israel, "You only have I chosen among all the

families of the earth; Therefore, I will punish you for all your iniquit-
ies" (Amos 3:2).

The choice is clear. Commitment to God is inseparable from commitment to righteousness. We must choose one side of the fence or the
other—hot or cold—but lukewarmness will get us nowhere. If you
have problems in the Christian life such as difficulty in prayer or in experiencing God's reality, examine your life to see if you are treating sin
as something trivial. To know God, we must be committed to what is
good, true, holy, and righteous. If you are clinging to a sin, even what
you regard as a minor sin, it will block your communion with God. "If
I regard wickedness in my heart, the Lord will not hear" (Ps.66:18).

Chapter 3

Riches, the Root of
Spiritual Dullness

Blind and deaf

The Lord Jesus repeatedly speaks of those who have eyes that do not see, and ears that do not hear. How has this come about? Why do some people have eyes, yet don't see spiritual things? Or ears, yet hear nothing in God's word? For such people, going to a Bible study would be as pointless as taking a blind man to watch a silent movie, or inviting someone who doesn't appreciate music to a music concert.

Jesus says that the Israelites, the people of God, have eyes that do not see, and ears that do not hear:

> Therefore I speak to them in parables; because while seeing they do not see, and while hearing they do not hear, nor do they understand. And in their case the prophecy of Isaiah is being fulfilled, which says, "You will keep on hearing, but will not understand; And you will keep on seeing, but will not perceive; For the heart of this people has become dull, And with their ears they scarcely hear, And they have closed their eyes lest they should see with their eyes, And hear with their ears, And understand with their heart and return, And I should heal them." (Mt.13:13-15, NASB)

But if their eyes should see and their ears hear, and if they return to God, He will heal them. The crucial issue is to be healed (to be saved), for you will die if you are not healed spiritually.

Jesus brings up the same point—seeing yet not seeing, hearing yet not hearing—in Mark 4:12 and 8:18, and Luke 8:10. John speaks of the Jews in similar terms in John 12:40 as does Paul in Acts 28:26 and Romans 11:8. This recurring theme in Scripture clearly indicates that we have to pay serious attention to the problem of spiritual blindness and deafness.

In Matthew 13 Jesus is quoting Isaiah, an Old Testament prophet. What was true of Israel in the time of Isaiah was later true of Israel in the time of Jesus and also true of the church today. The passage that Jesus quotes is Isaiah 6:10-11 (note the word "insensitive"):

> "Render the hearts of this people *insensitive*, their ears dull, and their eyes dim, Otherwise they might see with their eyes, hear with their ears, understand with their hearts, and return and be healed." Then I said, "Lord, how long?" And He answered, "Until cities are devastated and without inhabitant, houses are without people, and the land is utterly desolate." (Isaiah 6:10-11, NASB)

Destruction and desolation is the end result of blindness and deafness. The failure to be healed will lead to devastation.

Fat hearts

So why are they spiritually blind and deaf? What is the root cause of their disease? In the passage just quoted, NASB says that the hearts of the people have become "insensitive" (see italics). But the original word in Hebrew does not mean "insensitive" but "fat" (as preserved in KJV, "Make the heart of this people fat"). When we think of fat, we think of cholesterol deposits in the arteries that clog blood circulation and cause cardiac arrest.

Since Isaiah is not speaking in medical terms, we need to find clues that may explain what he means. The best commentary on the Bible is the Bible itself. One way of arriving at the meaning of a word in a verse is to see how the word is used elsewhere in the Bible. A useful tool for this is a concordance. Indeed Dt.31:20 uses the same Hebrew word for "fat" (see the italics):

> For when I bring them into the land flowing with milk and honey, which I swore to their fathers, and they have eaten and are satisfied and become *prosperous*, then they will turn to other gods and serve them, and spurn Me and break My covenant. (NASB)

Here we don't see the word "fat" because NASB translates the Hebrew word as "prosperous". The people of Israel were about to enter a land flowing with milk and honey. Like the Jews today, they were a hard-working people. When given fertile land and favorable circumstances, they become productive and prosperous. But God foresaw that when they become prosperous, they will turn away from Him and His covenant, and turn to other gods.

God was prophesying what was yet to happen, telling Moses what the Israelites will do later. They hadn't even yet entered the Promised Land but God had already foreseen that they will become prosperous in the land and will turn away from Him. God reads people like an open book. In the very next chapter, Moses says something similar:

> Then Jeshurun became fat and rebelled—you became fat, bloated, and gorged. He abandoned the God who made him and scorned the Rock of his salvation. (Dt.32:15, HCSB)

Jeshurun is another name for Israel, and ironically it means "righteous one". The Israelites were called to be righteous but they forsook God when they became prosperous. They even "scorned" (a strong word) the Rock of their salvation.

Moses wasn't talking about the Israelites in the third person. He was talking *directly* to them, telling them what they will do in the future. Sure enough, God's own people later turned their backs on Him when they became prosperous, in the way described by Isaiah. Their hearts grew fat, their eyes no longer saw, their ears no longer heard. They became spiritually sick, a most dangerous condition to be in. In fact Israel could not be healed until it was destroyed as a nation. The

Old Testament recounts for us the end result of their blindness and deafness: *destruction.*

Rebelliousness

One day the word of Yahweh came to Ezekiel, "Son of man, you are living among a rebellious house. They have eyes to see but do not see, and ears to hear but do not hear, for they are a rebellious house." (Eze.12:2) It was because of rebelliousness that the people had become blind and deaf, such are the dreadful consequences of prosperity. In Scripture, rebelliousness is punishable by death:

> If a man has a stubborn and rebellious son who does not obey his father and mother and will not listen to them when they discipline him, his father and mother shall take hold of him and bring him to the elders at the gate of his town. They shall say to the elders, "This son of ours is *stubborn and rebellious.* He will not obey us. He is a profligate and a drunkard." Then all the men of his town shall stone him to death. You must purge the evil from among you. All Israel will hear of it and be afraid. (Dt.21:18-21, NIV, italics added)

If a son is "stubborn and rebellious," not even his parents are to spare him the death penalty. Yet in the Bible there is not a single case, with one notable exception, in which a son is put to death with the consent of his parent or parents. Which parents, no matter how rebellious their son, would take him to the city gates to be put to death? No parent, I think, is capable of doing that. The only one who has ever used this Deuteronomic provision was God Himself, but *not* because of any rebelliousness on the part of His Son. The very next verse says:

> And if a man has committed a sin worthy of death, and he is put to death, and you hang him on a tree ... (Dt.21:22, NASB)

Paul links this verse to Jesus: "Cursed is everyone who hangs on a tree" (Gal.3:13). In the New Testament, the tree is a symbol of the cross. This shows God's absolute commitment to us, for He "did not spare his own Son but gave him up for us all" (Rom.8:32) even though we deserve death for our sins.

But that statement has a flip side: If God did not spare His own Son, neither will He spare us if we are rebellious. "For if God did not spare the natural branches, neither will he spare you" (Romans 11:21). The natural branches refer to Israel; the "you" refers to the Gentile Christians. We must not think that we, just because we are sons of God, will be spared by God no matter how unrighteously we live. God did not spare His own Son who was righteous. In the light of Scripture, neither will He spare you if you are rebellious, or if your eyes do not see and your ears do not hear.

Treasure on earth

So far in our survey of the Sermon on the Mount, we skipped over a key passage which we now bring up for discussion:

> Do not lay up for yourselves treasures upon earth, where moth and rust destroy, and where thieves break in and steal. But lay up for yourselves treasures in heaven, where neither moth nor rust destroys, and where thieves do not break in or steal; for where your treasure is, there will your heart be also. The lamp of the body is the eye; if therefore your eye is clear, your whole body will be full of light. But if your eye is bad, your whole body will be full of darkness. If therefore the light that is in you is darkness, how great is the darkness! No one can serve two masters; for either he will hate the one and love the other, or he will hold to one and despise the other. You cannot serve God and mammon. (Mt.6:19-24, NASB)

"Mammon" is an Aramaic word for riches and possessions, and includes things such as gold, silver, land, property. Aramaic, related to Hebrew, was the common language spoken in Palestine in the time of Jesus. He is saying that where your treasure is, there your heart will be. If you store your treasure on earth, your heart will be on earth. If you store your treasure in heaven, your heart will be on heaven. But you cannot be committed to two masters. You cannot serve God and mammon, for you must choose the one or the other. Dual commitment is not an option because it is partial commitment, and partial commitment is ultimately no commitment.

Superstition and the worship of mammon

In a TIME magazine article on the Bank of China building in Hong Kong, there is an interesting statement: "Together with the worship of mammon, belief in *feng shui* appears to be Hong Kong's dominant religion." The article is saying that Hong Kong's religion is the worship of mammon, money and possessions. A consequence of this is the widespread belief in *feng shui* or geomancy. *Feng shui*, literally "wind, water" in Chinese, is the practice of magic or spiritism in connection with land or geography. The *feng shui* masters were saying that the structure of this new building lacked good *feng shui* in terms of wind and water, or of the spirits associated with these elements.

I notice that those who love and worship mammon are inclined to be superstitious. This is true not only in Hong Kong but also in the West. In North America and other places, the newspapers have a *Daily Horoscopes* column. Many people do not start their day without consulting their horoscopes, to get advice from astrologers on what they should or should not do that day.

Superstition is everywhere. Some say it is bad luck to walk under a ladder or to encounter a black cat. Many consider the number 13 to be unlucky. Most apartment buildings don't have the 13th floor. When I was in Israel, I stayed with a friend who was living in building 13, on the 13th floor, in apartment 52, which is 4 x 13!

A false gospel: Believe in God and get rich!

As we shall see, the New Testament says a lot about riches *but in a negative tone*. That is because riches cause the heart to grow fat, leading to a spiritual disease that makes our eyes blind and our ears deaf. This is not a matter of theory but of reality. Unless we face this issue, there is no point in talking about commitment for we cannot commit to God and to riches at the same time.

Jim and Tammy Faye Bakker are two of many Christian leaders who twist the gospel to say that you can worship God and get rich (Jim Bakker has since rejected this false teaching). They teach not only that serving God is compatible with serving mammon, but that if you worship God, you will get lots of mammon! Hence believing in God is the way to get materially rich. Isn't this a wonderful gospel? If you preach it, you will get many converts.

There is some truth to this teaching but not in the way we expect. A businessman friend of mine whom I know very well came to know God some time back. Before he became a Christian, he had a business that was doing not too badly. He was making headway in his business but for a couple of years he was progressing slowly.

But when he became a Christian, his business took off like a rocket and he had to employ more people. Then an American company gave him exclusive rights to their products and to be their sole representative in his country. All their products had to be bought through him. The American company asked him to set up branches throughout the country to sell their products. So his small hole-in-the-wall business was poised to become a nationwide business. You would expect him to be happy. The Bakkers were right after all: believe in God and you will get rich!

I thank God that my friend was more discerning than that and was suspicious about what was going on. He said to me, "Before I became a Christian, I was always hoping for something like this to happen. But now that I'm a Christian, I'm not really happy about it." I asked him why he was unhappy, and he said, "Because I'm too busy to be quiet, to read my Bible, to pray." He then added, "I want to quit this business."

Satan tempts us with riches

What do you think of my friend's situation? If God was the one who made him successful in the first place, shouldn't he be happy about it? But he was not. Was he being ungrateful to God for the business boost? And was it a blessing from God in the first place?

The matter is not as straightforward as it may seem. Let me warn you that when you believe in God, Satan will try to tempt you with riches. What is the scriptural basis for saying this? As soon as Jesus got baptized, Satan offered him the world if he would only turn back from his commitment to God. We could imagine Satan saying to Jesus or to my businessman friend, "Don't be foolish. Let me give you the world and make you rich! You just got baptized but this won't nullify your baptism."

Satan knows that making you rich is the way to give you spiritual heart disease. What is more, he will disguise himself such that the undiscerning Christian will say, "God has blessed me!" Satan was trying to do this to my friend. After my friend got baptized, his business took off. But he felt that something was fishy because he knew that God doesn't work like that. He sensed that it was Satan who was giving him the world. Satan has the power to make you rich. There are no doubts about it. In fact Satan offered Jesus the whole world:

> The devil took him to a very high mountain and showed him all the kingdoms of the world and their glory. And he said to him, "All these I will give you, if you will fall down and worship me." (Mt.4:8-9)

How's that for an offer? Have you ever earned the whole world in a few seconds? What is your current salary? Even if you are paid well, that is peanuts compared to what Satan can give you. Ever since I came to know God, I have lost count of how many temptations have been put before me. I am amazed at the ways the world has been offered to me time and again. To this day I am still scratching my head, wondering where all these things came from, though I eventually rejected them.

The broad road

When I first came out of China, I was allowed to take ten Chinese dollars along with me; everything else had to be left behind. I was almost penniless. I arrived at Kowloon Station in Hong Kong. After having spent my money on the train fare, I was wondering how I was going to get to the hostel. So it was good that an elder from our church in Shanghai was waiting for me at the station and took me to the hostel.

Soon after arriving in Hong Kong, I was offered a full unconditional scholarship to study in the United States. I said to the one who was presenting me the offer: "Amazing! How did you hear about me? I just came out of China."

She said, "Oh, we have heard about you."

I asked, "What strings are attached? What are your conditions? What do you want from me for this scholarship?"

Can you imagine the United States government offering a scholarship to someone who had just come out of China? The offer came to me through a missionary acting on behalf of the American government.

She said, "There are no strings attached".

I was incredulous and asked, "You're offering me a scholarship to the United States with no strings attached? You must have something in mind. People don't give away money for nothing."

She said, "There are no conditions. You don't need to repay any of this. We don't want anything from you. The only thing we ask of you is that you be a friend of the United States."

"Is that all?"

"Yes, that's all."

"I just came out of China, so how am I going to enter the United States?" (At that time there were no diplomatic relations between the two countries.)

"Leave it to us. We'll take care of your visas and papers."

"Okay, another thing. If I study medicine, that may take seven or eight years. Do you know how much that costs?"

"No problem."

"Maybe I'll go for a Ph.D., ten years."

"Ten years is fine."

"Which university will I be going to?"

"Any university you want."

If I picked Harvard, that would be okay. If I picked MIT, that would be okay too. Amazing! The government will take care of everything. The only condition is to be a friend of the United States.

I said, "Look, I'm just a young man who came out of China. I'm a nobody. Why is my friendship important to you?"

"Because we know that you will become a leader of your people."

"Well, I must say that you are very clever."

It is clever to buy a friend in his time of financial need. Jesus talks about making friends by means of unrighteous mammon (Lk.16:9). Making friends by means of money is important in the world.

Even if I studied ten years at a university, the total cost in those days would have been tens of thousands of dollars. That's peanuts to a government that puts billions of dollars into foreign aid. And those tens of thousands would be spread over several years. The actual cost per year would be only a few thousand in terms of the dollar fifty years ago. That would be a drop in the bucket for a government budget of billions of dollars. And with that they can buy a friend for the future.

I am still wondering why they think I was going to be a leader. Was it in terms of ability? Their eyesight is interesting too, being very sharp in the ways of the world. As Jesus says in Luke 16:8, "the sons of this age are wiser in relation to their own kind than the sons of light"—the people of the world are wiser and shrewder than Christians. I have observed that non-Christians are wise and clever in what they do.

So the world was offered to me on a platter, just like that. She said, "Do you accept the offer?" I said, "I do nothing apart from God's instructions. I will ask Him if I may accept the offer, and then get back to you." She said, "All right."

I went back to the hostel and knelt before God, saying, "Lord, is this from you?" At that time I had no job or money. I had just come out of China, and there were vast numbers of refugees like me in Hong Kong, also jobless and living in poverty. The situation in Hong Kong was terrible and chaotic. Yet I was given a golden opportunity probably offered to few people in the world. I prayed before God and He said "no". I had no job or money but *no* means *no*.

When this missionary saw me a few days later and asked for my decision, I said, "I deeply appreciate your kind offer and I thank you. But my God does not allow me to take the scholarship."

The missionary was surprised but showed no anger or unhappiness. She simply said, "Any time you want this scholarship, it's yours."

"Really? Even in ten years' time?"

"Yes, even in ten years' time. The scholarship is always open to you. If you should ever change your mind about the offer, contact me and you will have this scholarship."

But I never took it. Instead I walked on a hard road of poverty. For many years after, I would often live from hand to mouth and did not have a cent in my pocket. But I have never regretted my decision or felt the temptation to accept the offer. Since my Lord said *no*, that was the end of the matter. If I had taken the easy road, I would have had a good life with everything paid for. But this will come at an enormous price: I would have lost all spiritual power. My heart would have grown fat; my eyes would have been blind; my ears, deaf. I would be useless to God. There is the broad and easy road of mammon versus the narrow and hard road of following God.

I have turned my back on the world many times and I don't regret it. When I was about to finish my studies in London, another offer came along: my professor proposed that I do a doctorate. Once again, opportunities opened up before me. He said I could take up a teaching assistantship at the university. It seems that he wanted to groom me to be his successor and to take over his post at the department one day. I thanked him but told him I wasn't interested in the doctorate or in pursuing that line of study anymore.

Again and again at decisive points in my life, there was a fork in the road that forced me to choose between the narrow road and the broad road, between God and mammon. Each time I was walking on a difficult road of following God. It would have been much easier to take the broad road but Jesus says you cannot serve God and mammon.

Blessed are the poor in spirit

We continue our study of what the Bible says about riches. The Bible has a lot to say on this topic, yet it is one that is seldom taught in the church from the perspective of Scripture. Today you seldom hear a sermon on what the Bible *really* says about riches. That is because no pastor wants to offend his hearers. As we shall see, when the New Testament speaks on the subject, it has a negative tone towards riches. If we are to be faithful to God's word and to God himself, we need to examine the matter with an open and honest heart.

The first statement in the Sermon on the Mount is, "Blessed are the poor in spirit, for theirs is the kingdom of heaven" (Mt.5:3). Note the two words "in spirit". Many people are happy with "in spirit" because to them it spiritualizes away literal poverty. A spiritually poor person, it is hoped, can still have lots of money. But such an attempt to justify riches will not work.

Whenever Jesus uses the word "poor" in the four gospels outside this verse (Mt.5:3), he always refers to literal poverty, not spiritual poverty.[4] This is seen for example in Mt.19:21 ("sell what you possess and give to the poor") and even in Mt.11:5: "the blind see, the lame walk, those with skin diseases are healed, the deaf hear, the dead are raised, and the poor are told the good news." It is remarkable that the gospel, the good news, is preached to the poor.

Here Jesus is quoting Isaiah 61:1 of the Old Testament. In the Old Testament, "poor" always refers to those who live in literal poverty, not spiritual poverty. We cannot survey the Old Testament here, but if you look up "poor" in the Old Testament section of a concordance, you will see that it always refers to the literal poor. For example, Amos 2:6-7 says that poor and needy are sold for a pair of sandals:

> The LORD says: I will not relent from punishing Israel for three crimes, even four, because they sell a righteous person for silver and a needy person for a pair of sandals. They trample the heads of the poor on the dust of the ground and block the path of the needy.

---

[4] Matthew 11:5; 19:21; 26:11; Mark 10:21; 12:43; 14:7; Luke 4:18; 6:20; 7:22; 14:13; 14:21; 16:20,22; 18:22; 21:3; John 12:8.

Two chapters later, we see again the exploitation of the poor:

> Listen to this message, you cows of Bashan who are on the hill of
> Samaria, women who oppress the poor and crush the needy, who
> say to their husbands, "Bring us something to drink." (Amos 4:1)

In prophetic sarcasm, Amos calls the rich women the cows of Bashan.
Bashan is a region in Israel with good grazing land where cows get fat.
God will judge these rich women who were oppressing the poor:

> Therefore, because you trample on the poor and exact a grain tax
> from him, you will never live in the houses of cut stone you have
> built; you will never drink the wine from the lush vineyards you
> have planted. For I know your crimes are many and your sins in-
> numerable. They oppress the righteous, take a bribe, and deprive the
> poor of justice at the gates. (Amos 5:11-12, all verses from HCSB)

Why the recurring theme of the oppression of the poor? Amos is
warning that Israel will be destroyed as a nation because it has been
oppressing the poor. That is the point. God will pour forth destruction
on Israel. The exploitation of the poor is seen again three chapters
later, in Amos 8:4 ("you who trample on the needy and do away with
the poor of the land") and 8:6 ("that we may buy the poor for silver
and the needy for a pair of sandals"). In the next verse God says, "I will
never forget all their deeds" (v.7) and then spells out in terrifying detail
the coming destruction of Israel as a nation (v.8ff). God feels strongly
about the treatment of the poor.

Let us summarize. Jesus says that the gospel is preached to the poor.
In saying this, he is quoting from the Old Testament. Whenever the
Old Testament speaks of the poor, it always refers to those who live in
material poverty, not spiritual poverty.

We can confirm our understanding of "poor in spirit" by comparing Scripture with Scripture. What Jesus says in Matthew 5 about the
poor is repeated in Luke 6:20-25:

> [20] Looking at his disciples, he said: "Blessed are you who are poor, for
> yours is the kingdom of God. [21] Blessed are you who hunger now, for

you will be satisfied. Blessed are you who weep now, for you will laugh. [22] Blessed are you when men hate you, when they exclude you and insult you and reject your name as evil, because of the Son of Man. [23] Rejoice in that day and leap for joy, because great is your reward in heaven. For that is how their fathers treated the prophets. [24] But woe to you who are rich, for you have already received your comfort. [25] Woe to you who are well fed now, for you will go hungry. Woe to you who laugh now, for you will mourn and weep." (Luke 6:20-25, NIV)

Note the two underlined statements. Exegetically, if the "poor" in v.20 are the *spiritually* poor (as supposed by most Christians), it would follow that the "rich" in v.24 are by correspondence the *spiritually* rich. But if that is the case, why would Jesus say, "Woe to you who are rich"? The word "woe" would be totally inappropriate because the spiritually rich are blessed in God's eyes, not cursed. Hence Jesus must be referring to the *literal* rich in v.24 and the *literal* poor in v.20. We cannot turn "poor in spirit" into a spiritualized poverty.

Why then does Jesus use "poor in spirit" instead of "poor" in Mt. 5:3? That is because literal poverty does not in itself guarantee God's blessing. Many poor people love riches as much as rich people do. It's not only the rich but equally the poor who are greedy. Jesus speaks of "poor in spirit" because merely being poor is not good enough. There has to be the spiritual willingness to be poor in the sense of not being greedy for riches. If you are poor yet long for riches, you are not fundamentally different from the rich. The only difference is that the rich have money and the poor do not. The poor hope to get rich one day, perhaps through the lottery. If their heart's desire is for riches, they won't be blessed by God either.

We can put the matter like this: You can be poor without being righteous or spiritual, but you cannot be righteous or spiritual without being poor.

Practical living

Most people see nothing wrong with loving money. This way of thinking has been ingrained in us all our lives. "I love money but I also love

God. What's wrong with that?" This is one of the biggest obstacles to commitment.

Jesus tells us not to store up riches on earth for ourselves, yet we do this thing every day. When I get sick, how will I pay the hospital bills? I also need a house to live in. I need to buy furniture. Am I going to sit on the floor? When you get married or have a baby, you will rack up expenses. You need to save up now. No money means no marriage, no baby, no house. When you reach retirement, who will support you? You can't live off your parents because they may need your support. What about your children's education? If you don't save up now, how are you going to pay for all these things?

And shouldn't we be practical in life? Why live in the clouds? We have to keep our feet on solid ground. Without money, we won't survive in the world. It's fine to talk about total commitment to God, but since we live in the world, we have to be realistic. When you get on the bus, you have to pay the fare. Are you going to wait for a kind person to pay for your journey?

So we reason: "The Christian life is not practical. But we are practical people who know the importance of money though we'll try not to love money too much. The Lord says not to store up riches on earth, but that's not possible in the modern age. Who doesn't have a bank account these days? You can't even pay your bills without an account. A bank account has money, so that would be storing up riches, right?"

So how do we put into practice the Lord's teaching of not storing up riches? We need to think deeply on this. In the next chapter we will continue on this topic.

A personal sharing: Jesus' teaching really works

Meanwhile I can testify that I have lived according to the principle of not storing up riches, and I am still around! I know first-hand that it works. Ever since I came to know God, I have never saved up anything from my earnings to this day. In any case, I didn't earn anything worth talking about. In my student days, when I was serving in a church in London, I wasn't paid for years of work. Though I led the Bible study every week, preached sometimes two Sundays a month, led some other groups, and spoke at church conferences, I didn't receive a penny of pay for several years of work. And I didn't seek any pay either.

Later when I served in a church in Liverpool, I also received no pay. I declined a salary and was supported by voluntary named offerings. Most of the church people didn't know I was supported only by such offerings. They didn't know that the money put into the offering box didn't come to me, and that I wasn't paid by the church.

Before moving to Canada, I had to declare my net worth as a new immigrant. I had to fill out a form, yet I had no money to declare. I thought to myself, "If I'm entering Canada and can't even declare a few dollars of net worth, they will wonder what kind of immigrant I am." If I put down $50, the immigration officer will think, "This guy has a wife and a kid. And this family arrives in Canada with $50?"

I said, "Lord, what will I put on this form?" After waiting before God, I said, "If it's alright with you, I will put down $1,000 by faith." I didn't have $1,000 Canadian, but I declared the amount by faith.

When I arrived in Montreal, the immigration officer asked me, "You put down $1,000 in your form. Have you got it?" I said, "Hold on, let me count." I pulled out everything I got. I asked my wife to put everything on the table. We counted $1,004. That was our total worth. In all the years of serving in the church, I was able to put $1,004 on the table, most of which had been given to us as farewell gifts just before we left Liverpool.

When you move to a new country, you need to buy things. Coming from England, we didn't have clothes or boots suitable for the Canadian winter. These things are expensive but God supplied us with everything we needed.

We have never saved up a reserve from our income. At the end of every month we would be down to zero, and we want to keep it that way. Does being penniless mean that we are in financial difficulty? Not at all! In fact we have never lacked anything.

If you don't live the Bible, how can you teach the Bible? If I haven't lived the Bible, I wouldn't be able to expound this teaching on riches with any conviction.

Chapter 4

Poverty, Spirituality, and Lordship

Why is it that we cannot be righteous or spiritual without being poor? If you are at all serious about the spiritual life, you may find the question disconcerting. When Jesus told the rich young ruler of the high cost of inheriting eternal life—"sell your possessions and give to the poor" and "come, follow me"—the young man could not take it (Mt.19:21-22). It got stuck in his throat. He wanted eternal life but the price was too high. Maybe it is too high for some of us too.

But I can't make it any easier for you because I don't have the authority to say, "Enter the kingdom of heaven by the back door because it is hard getting in through the front door."

Yet it is fair to ask: What is the scriptural basis for saying we cannot be righteous or spiritual without being poor? This is what we will be looking at in this chapter, especially in the light of Jesus' teaching in the gospel of Luke.

Right from the start of Luke's gospel, we read, "He has filled the hungry with good things but has sent the rich away empty" (Lk.1:53). Hence, already in the first chapter of Luke, there is a certain rejection of the rich. The rich are sent away empty with no spiritual blessings from God. This is hinted in Luke 4:18 from a different angle:

> The Spirit of the Lord is upon me, because he has anointed me to
> proclaim good news to the poor. He has sent me to proclaim liberty

to the captives and recovering of sight to the blind, to set at liberty
those who are oppressed. (Luke 4:18, ESV)

The gospel is preached to the poor rather than the rich. One could say
that the gospel has the poor as its specific object. This is seen again
three chapters later:

> Go back and report to John what you have seen and heard: The
> blind receive sight, the lame walk, those who have leprosy are
> cured, the deaf hear, the dead are raised, and the good news is
> preached to the poor. (Luke 7:22, NIV)

The rejection of the rich is seen also in Luke 6:24-25:

> But woe to you who are rich, for you have already received your
> comfort. Woe to you who are well fed now, for you will go hungry.
> Woe to you who laugh now, for you will mourn and weep. (NIV)

A woe is a curse, and is the opposite of blessing. The contrast between
woe and blessing is brought out in the immediate context: verses 20 to
23 are addressed to the blessed whereas verses 24 to 26 are addressed
to those under judgment. The "woe to you" condemnations will be
fully realized on the day of judgment.

The Parable of the Rich Fool

Continuing in Luke's gospel, we come to the parable of the rich fool
(Lk.12:16-21). In the parable, a farmer is getting richer and richer. His
harvest is so plentiful that he has run out of space to store his crops, so
he pulls down his barns and build bigger ones. Here is the first half of
the parable:

> The ground of a certain rich man yielded an abundant harvest. He
> thought to himself, "What shall I do? I have no place to store my
> crops." Then he said, "This is what I'll do. I will tear down my barns
> and build bigger ones, and there I will store my surplus grain. And
> I'll say to myself, 'You have plenty of grain laid up for many years.
> Take life easy; eat, drink and be merry.'" (Luke 12:16-19, NIV)

In your mind it must have been God who blessed him with riches because a good harvest is a blessing from God. This is not a problem. The problem isn't with the rich man's harvest but with what he does with his wealth: he stores it up *for himself* (v.21). The problem is not in having a good income but what one does with it.

The rich man looks at his wealth with self-satisfaction and says to himself, "You have plenty of good things laid up for years. Take life easy; eat, drink and be merry". Little does he know that he will die that very night:

> God said to him, "You fool! This very night your life will be demanded from you. Then who will get what you have prepared for yourself?" This is how it will be with whoever stores up things for himself but is not rich toward God. (Luke 12:20-21, NIV)

The problem with the rich man is that he stores up riches for himself and lives for himself. What Jesus says in Mt.16:26 is entirely relevant here: "For what will it profit a man if he gains the whole world and forfeits his soul? Or what shall a man give in return for his soul?"

In England, when rich people die, their estates are often listed in the newspapers. Person so-and-so has left behind £100,000; another has left behind £500,000. For those without heirs, presumably their wealth will be transferred to the state. So why did they store up riches that they could no longer use? Everything is left behind when they die, as in the case of the rich fool. Indeed God says to him, "Who will get what you have prepared for yourself?" (Lk.12:20).

Sell your possessions

In the same chapter a few verses later, the Lord Jesus again draws the contrast between earthly riches and heavenly treasure:

> [32] Do not be afraid, little flock, for your Father has been pleased to give you the kingdom. [33] Sell your possessions and give to the poor. Provide purses for yourselves that will not wear out, a treasure in heaven that will not be exhausted, where no thief comes near and no

moth destroys. [34] For where your treasure is, there your heart will be also. (Luke 12:32-34, NIV)

Verse 33 ("sell your possessions and give to the poor") is the part that sticks in our throats, as it was in the case of the rich young ruler (Lk.18:22-23). What Jesus required of the rich young ruler—to sell his possessions—applies to us too because v.33 is addressed to the "little flock," that is, the disciples.

So far we have stayed in Luke's gospel, yet in that one gospel we have already seen much penetrating teaching on the subject of riches. Let us continue in Luke's gospel, to yet another passage about riches:

He also said to the one who had invited Him, "When you give a lunch or a dinner, don't invite your friends, your brothers, your relatives, or your rich neighbors, because they might invite you back, and you would be repaid. On the contrary, when you host a banquet, invite those who are poor, maimed, lame, or blind. And you will be blessed, because they cannot repay you; for you will be repaid at the resurrection of the righteous." (Luke 14:12-14, HCSB)

Give to those who cannot repay you. In Chinese custom, if you give me something worth $100, it would be proper of me to give you back something of similar value. But Jesus says that when you give, seek out those who have no means of giving back. Seek out a poor man and invite him to lunch because he won't be able to return your generosity.

This is irrational by the standards of the world. But the whole point is that "you will be repaid at the resurrection of the righteous" (v.14). Again we see the matter of storing up treasure in heaven. If the one you invite for lunch gives you something back, you have already gained your reward. But if he cannot give you anything back, you are going to have an eternal reward. Do we understand this way of thinking? It takes a lot of faith and commitment to fulfill this teaching because it touches our wallets.

In the same chapter we see yet another statement on possessions: "No one of you can be my disciple who does not give up all his possessions" (Lk.14:33). This statement is so clear as to require no further exposition, so it is up to us to take it or leave it.

The true riches are eternal

Continuing in Luke, we come to another passage about riches. Note the important words "true riches" and "of your own" (see italics):

> "So if you have not been trustworthy in handling worldly wealth, who will trust you with *true riches*? And if you have not been trustworthy with someone else's property, who will give you property *of your own*? No servant can serve two masters. Either he will hate the one and love the other, or he will be devoted to the one and despise the other. You cannot serve both God and Money." The Pharisees, who loved money, heard all this and were sneering at Jesus. (Luke 16:11-14, NIV)

The Pharisees were highly religious people. In fact *Pharisee* means "pious one". In the days of Jesus, they were the defenders of the Law. Yet these religious leaders loved money as do many Christians today.

When the Pharisees heard what Jesus said about riches, they scoffed at him because they considered his teaching to be too radical to be taken seriously. His teaching on riches is indeed hard to swallow, as we have seen throughout the gospel of Luke.

Yet in this passage Jesus also talks about the "true riches" which are eternal and do not pass away, in contrast to the earthly riches which will pass away. I know someone who made a lot of money investing in stocks and shares, but when the market crashed in Hong Kong, he lost everything! He was a millionaire one day, penniless the next. That's why Jesus says earthly treasure is not the "true riches". You came into the world without a penny, and you will leave the world without a penny. In the intervening years of your life, you are only a steward of the money put into your hands. One day you will leave everything behind. If you don't give up your riches now, you will give them up in the future. You might say, "That's fine with me, I'll give up my riches when I die." But then you won't have the "true riches" either.

To have the true riches, you must prove your faithfulness in handling what is in your hands right now. If you have not been faithful with unrighteous mammon, how can you be entrusted with the true riches that God is ready to give you and which are your own? This is an exhortation to manage our income and possessions as faithful stewards.

Transient treasure

There was an incident in USA in which many had their safety deposit boxes stolen. The thieves dug a tunnel under the bank, breached the walls of the safety deposit area, and emptied all the deposit boxes. Everything was gone, from jewelry to bond certificates. In this world, nothing is safe.

I myself came from a fairly well-to-do family but we lost everything when the communists took over China. My father came out of China with one suitcase and so did I (separately). But everything else was gone. Being a young man at the time, I didn't really lose much because I hadn't earned anything. But everything that my father had acquired by hard work over the years was gone. We were hardly alone in this situation, for there were millions who had lost everything in China.

Putting one's trust in transient riches is the mistake Jesus warns us not to make. We just read in Lk.16:12 that your earthly riches don't belong to you permanently; they only pass through your hands. At the present time, they are yours in trust. God allows you to have the riches as a steward, and He can take them away any time, as in the case of the rich fool.

Our life is from God

The life you have, even the breath you have, is yours only because God allows you to have it. Psalm 36:9 says, "With you is the fountain of life". Your life is not your own, and God can take it away tonight, tomorrow, or the day after. We have no power to hold on to our lives, and when God decides it is time for us to go, no one can stop that.

In Liverpool I got asthma from the air pollution there. When I got my first asthma attack, I didn't know what the problem was. For the first time it dawned on me that I depend on just one breath to live. When I couldn't breathe, I didn't know what was happening to me. I was fighting to get one breath of air into my lungs. Asthma sufferers would know the horror of this situation. It seemed that every breath I got might be my last. I was wondering if I was going to survive the night. I didn't wake up my wife because she needed her sleep, so I struggled through the night by myself. When she saw me in the morning, she was horrified because my face had turned blue. She immediately rushed off to get a doctor.

We live one breath at a time. If someone is strangling us, we would be dead in a minute or two. Our life hangs on one breath. If our lives are given to us in trust, how much more our possessions. On that Day when you and I stand before God, we will have to give an account of how we lived this life and used our possessions. We need to see that our possessions do not belong to us. On the other hand, the life and the riches in the kingdom of God that will be given to us at the judgment will truly belong to us. Once God gives them, He will never take them back. These riches will be entrusted to us as truly our own ("your own," Lk.16:12).

Through the eye of a needle

Continuing in Luke's gospel, we come to a well-known passage in Luke 18:24-25:

> Jesus looked at him and said, "How hard it is for the rich to enter the kingdom of God! Indeed, it is easier for a camel to go through the eye of a needle than for a rich man to enter the kingdom of God."

If you are rich, how hard will it be for you to enter the kingdom of God? The biblical answer is: harder than for a camel to go through the eye of a needle! In other words, impossible! You cannot get into the kingdom until God does the impossible in you: slim down the camel until it becomes a strand of thread.

The disciples are astonished at this statement, saying, "Who then can be saved?" (v.26). Jesus answers, "What is impossible with men is possible with God". God can transform a rich man into a poor man, slimming him down so that he can go through the eye of a needle. We see this in the case of Zacchaeus:

> There was a man named Zacchaeus. He was a chief tax collector and was rich ... And when Jesus came to the place, he looked up and said to him, "Zacchaeus, hurry and come down, for I must stay at your house today." ... Zacchaeus stood and said to the Lord, "Behold, Lord, the half of my goods I give to the poor. And if I have defrauded anyone of anything, I restore it fourfold." And Jesus said to him, "Today salvation has come to this house, since he also is a son of Abraham." (Lk.19:2ff, ESV)

Salvation has come to the house of Zacchaeus! How has this come about? It is seen in his pledge to give half his possessions to the poor. This is a miracle that makes a rich man a poor man! You might say that Zacchaeus still has the other half for himself. Not quite so, because the problem is that he had cheated many. He will give half his possess-ions to the poor and use the other half as restitution to those he had cheated. In fact he offers them a fourfold repayment. By the time he is done with the restitution and has nothing left, you could say that the camel has slimmed down into a strand of thread. Now he can go through the eye of a needle.

Abraham's wealth

Some will argue that God wants us to be rich because Abraham was rich, and more than that, Abraham was a man who walked with God. This argument gives no end of comfort to those who wish to salve their conscience over their riches. But the argument runs into obstacles.

Firstly, the Old Testament functions by a different standard from the New Testament. It was an earthly standard in which all blessings were earthly blessings whereas in the New Testament, all blessings are spiritual blessings. In fact the whole Ephesians chapter 1 elaborates on the wonderful truth that God has "blessed us in Christ with every spiritual blessing in the heavenly places" (v.3). By contrast, the Old Testament blessings were mainly those of health, riches, and long life. Israel was promised earthly prosperity and a good harvest under the condition of obeying God. These earthly blessings were promised to Israel, the earthly people of God.

Abraham was rich, yet he also waged war against kings. This kind of thing is not permissible for Christians to do as a church (cf. Mt.26:52, "those who take up the sword will perish by the sword"). We cannot as a church and for the church take up literal arms against unrighteousness. But Abraham did something like that. It is exegetically invalid to argue for riches from the case of Abraham because he belonged to an earlier age and covenant. If we say that we can in the matter of money take Abraham as a standard for the New Testament, then it would be permissible for the church to go to war and kill. But if it's not right for us as a church to wage war as Abraham did (in his case, to rescue Lot), is it valid for us who are under the new covenant to base our view of riches on the old covenant?

Secondly, Abraham did not pursue riches. It was God who gave him his riches (Gen.24:35). Even if God makes us rich today, it doesn't mean that under the New Testament we are entitled to store it up for ourselves, as we see in the parable of the rich fool. The problem with the rich fool was not that he became rich (it was God who gave him a good harvest) but that he stored up riches for himself.

If one day you become rich through an inheritance, you could rightly say it was God who made you rich. You didn't work for it and it wasn't your fault that you are named the beneficiary in the deceased man's will. It's not your fault that you suddenly received a few million dollars. The question is what you do with it.

Thirdly, unusual for a rich man, Abraham never cared for riches, as we see in Hebrews 11 (vv.9,10,15,16). He was not interested in the things of the world but was looking to the eternal city with foundations, whose architect and builder is God. His heart was set on a better country, the heavenly kingdom.

This God-centered attitude was characteristic of Abraham. He was so devoted to God that when God asked him to offer up his son Isaac, he was willing. His son meant more to him than all his riches, yet he was willing to give up everything, even his own son, for God. If we have that kind of devotion to God, then perhaps we could start talking about using Abraham as a standard.

Riches: A source of security

We see from Scripture that we cannot be spiritual or righteous without being poor. The danger of riches is that we are going to depend on them for our security. Why do people want to get rich in the first place? The main reason is security.

How much do you trust in God? If God told you to, would you dare walk through a forest populated by wild tigers while trusting only in God? You might say, "I trust in God but tigers have teeth, so I am not sure if the arm of God is strong enough to protect me from the teeth of tigers." You would feel more secure with a high-power rifle in your hand. Then you can keep your finger on the trigger while trekking through the forest. Where are you putting your trust? In your weapon.

We might say: "We mustn't tempt God. Trusting solely in God is to tempt Him. You shouldn't make God do for you what you can do for yourself. So before entering the forest, I will buy a powerful rifle with a telescope and rapid repetition for if I misfire, reloading could be fatal!" So you put your trust in your rifle. If God tells you to go without it, you will say, "Lord, the world is just too dangerous."

Most households in the United States own guns. The right to own firearms is written in the constitution of the United States of America. Some people own so many guns that they practically run an arsenal. During a visit to Florida, when I was looking for swimming and diving gear, I walked into a shop that sold not only what I was looking for but also firearms. It carried machine guns, rifles, and pistols of every description. I was looking at these weapons with much fascination, some of which I had never seen before. A salesman came up to me and asked if I would like to buy a gun. I could even try it out at the back of the store!

I once visited a friend in Los Angeles. When evening came, I said to him, "How about going for a walk in the park?"

He said, "A walk in the park? It's already evening. No one in his right mind goes for a walk in the park at this time!"

"What is the purpose of a park if you can't walk in it?"

"We walk at daytime, not in the evening."

Seeing my disappointment, he said, "Okay, we'll go for a walk. But if you don't mind, I'll take along my gun."

"A gun? Just for a walk in the park? But if it makes you feel safer, take it along."

So he brought his gun along. I was relaxing in the park while he was getting nervous. Every time someone walked behind us, he would look back with his gun ready. So I said, "If this is going to make you a nervous wreck, let's go home." Anyone who wants to rob me must have poor eyesight. He can have the $10 in my pocket if he wants it.

Jesus as our Lord

To understand why the Bible says we cannot serve riches, we need to consider the meaning of the title "Lord". It is a frequent title of Jesus in the New Testament. Jesus is Lord because "God has made him both Lord and Christ" (Acts 2:36).

When I address someone as Lord or Master, what does it say about my relationship to him? That I am his servant. Christians address Jesus as Lord, but in what sense is he their Lord? Do you see yourself as a servant? Most of us have never been servants, so we use terms such as "servant" with little understanding of its meaning or significance.

The title "Lord" expresses power and authority—not physical power fundamentally but the power of control. If you call someone "Lord" you are acknowledging his authority to control your life. Conversely, if you don't acknowledge Jesus' right to control your life, you shouldn't call him "Lord" or you would be making it an empty title, much like what we said earlier about a constitutional monarch. Many Christians call Jesus "Lord" as a courtesy or traditional title but without giving him control of their lives.

No one can say "Jesus is Lord" except by the Holy Spirit (1Cor. 12:3). It is the Spirit's inner work that transforms our lives. Just as the rich young ruler cannot enter the kingdom unless he is transformed by

God's power, so you and I cannot call Jesus "Lord" from our hearts except by the Holy Spirit.

The Greek word for "Lord" (*kyrios*) also means the owner of a slave. That is why a slave would call his master "Lord." You cannot rightly call Jesus "Lord" unless you are his servant or slave. In the New Testament, "servant" and "slave" are the same word in Greek (*doulos*).

What is a slave? Oxford Dictionary defines a slave as "a person who is owned by another and has to serve him." Applying this to us in regard to the Lord Jesus, it means that you can rightly call Jesus "Lord" only if he truly owns you; otherwise he is not your Lord. Harper's Bible Dictionary defines slavery as "the total subjection of one person to another." If you are not totally subjected to Jesus, you cannot call him "Lord".

Slavery in New Testament times

Slavery was common in New Testament times. Socially and economically, Roman society was built on a system of slavery. Slavery was the foundation of that society. All kinds of people could become slaves. A slave may be skilled or unskilled. He may be a lawyer, a doctor, an engineer, or a common laborer. Slavery covered the whole spectrum of society and all professions, from the skilled to the unskilled.

There are three ways a person can become a slave:

1. Captured in war

The first way one can become a slave is to be captured in war. Many slaves in New Testament times were prisoners of war. Anyone could be captured and become a slave irrespective of his profession or social standing. The Romans would tie three lances together to form a *yoke* (an archway), and the prisoners of war were made to pass under it in a ceremony called "passing under the yoke." In the ceremony, all who passed under the yoke became slaves.

The Roman army, like most armies at the time, would take their prisoners of war back to Rome or some other city, and sell them as slaves to civilian buyers. The profit they made from selling the captives helped to fund the army. The captives were taken to the central market in Rome or some other city, and sold at a fixed price or auctioned to the highest bidder. The buyer would then own them as his slaves. The slaves had been bought with a price, and they now belong to someone.

2. Born of slave parents

The second way a person can become a slave is to be born to a slave. If one's mother is a slave, he would be born a slave.

3. Sold into slavery

The third way a person can become a slave is to be sold into slavery. If the parents of a boy or girl are poor, they might sell their child into slavery to repay debts or earn money for necessities. Some poor families had lots of children and they would sometimes sell their children into slavery. If they had no children to sell, they would sometimes sell themselves into slavery.

Three metaphors of slavery

In the New Testament, all three ways of becoming a slave apply to us metaphorically: First, we become slaves of sin by being captured into sin. Second, we were born of parents who were themselves slaves of sin. Third, we sold ourselves into slavery to sin, willingly or unwillingly.

The first metaphor, becoming a slave through captivity, is mentioned in 2Pet.2:19 which speaks of us being overcome by sin and becoming slaves of sin. We likewise become slaves of the devil by being captured by him (2Tim.2:26). But there is hope for us because God has freed us from slavery to sin by defeating Satan and the domain of darkness (Col.1:13), moving us from being under Satan's ownership to Christ's ownership.

The second metaphor, slavery through birth, is explained by Paul in the whole section in Galatians 4:21-31.

The third metaphor, being sold into slavery, is seen in both the Old and New Testaments. Exodus 21:7-11 discusses the case of a child who is sold into slavery for debt repayment. Exodus 22:3 tells of a thief who was sold into slavery because he had no money to repay what he had stolen. First Samuel 2:5 (and similarly Lev.25:47ff) tells of one who sold himself into slavery because of poverty or famine.

The third metaphor, being sold into slavery, is prominent in the New Testament, notably in Romans 6, especially verses 16 to 22. But verse 22 gives us the hope of freedom: "But now that you have been set free from sin and have become *slaves of God*, the fruit you get leads to sanctification and its end, eternal life."

We were formerly slaves of sin, but in the new life we are slaves of God and bear fruit for righteousness. Our earlier statement, that we cannot be righteous without being poor, brings us to this crucial point about slavery: Under the law, *a slave owns nothing*. Everything a slave has, including his own life, belongs to his master. If you are a slave of Jesus Christ, everything that you have, down to the last penny, belongs to him, not to yourself. A slave is poor for the very reason that he doesn't own anything, not even his own life.

Slaves in Roman society were given provisions

Yet in Roman society, a slave was often given money for personal use. He could use it to buy personal items such as clothes. A master would not want his slave to walk around in rags because that would disgrace the master's name. He wants his slave to be properly clothed so that his friends would say, "His slave is well looked after." The Romans are like the Chinese and the Japanese in attaching importance to "face". The master doesn't want to be known as a bad slave owner, but as one whose slave is diligent, well fed, healthy, and properly looked after.

The master would give his slave some pocket money that he was free to use as he pleased. He could buy himself a cake, or invest the money, or loan it out to others. A slave was free to use the money, yet strictly speaking and under the law, the money still belonged to the master. Anything he bought with the money, perhaps a garment, belonged to his master, not himself. Strictly speaking and under the law, any profit he made by investing the money belonged to his master. In other words, a slave was poor by definition because he owned nothing under the law.

Yet in Roman society you couldn't always tell a slave from a free man if he walked by you in public, not even by the way he dressed, for there was often no mark to identify him as a slave. In Hong Kong today where many Filipino women work as domestic helpers, you often cannot tell if one is a maid or a tourist or an investor just by her appearance.

We are slaves of God

What is the basis for saying we cannot be spiritual or righteous without being poor? The answer is that we cannot be spiritual or righteous without being *a slave of God*. Everything we have, including our lives, belongs to God. True commitment involves a total surrender of our lives and everything we have to God.

If you are a committed Christian, you would acknowledge that every cent in your bank account, every cent you earn, belongs to God, and that you are not at liberty to do with the money as you please. When you give God full control of your life, you will ask Him what you are to do with the money. Perhaps someone has a financial need. When I give to a needy person, ultimately it is not I but God who gives him the money, through me. I take no self-satisfaction in giving to the needy, nor do I say to myself, "I am righteous for giving him $100." We have nothing to boast about because a slave has nothing to boast about. There are no grounds for self-righteousness. Yet you will be commended by God when He says, "You did the right thing. Giving that $100 was in full accord with my will." You will receive praise from God even though you have nothing in yourself to boast about.

Total commitment requires the willingness to be a slave of God. "You have been bought with a price; therefore glorify God in your body" (1Cor.6:20); "You were bought with a price" (7:23).

Slavery and friendship

> Greater love has no one than this, that he lay down his life for his
> friends. You are my friends if you do what I command. I no longer
> call you servants, because a servant does not know his master's busi-
> ness. Instead, I have called you friends, for everything that I learned
> from my Father I have made known to you. (John 15:13-15, NIV)

Jesus redeemed us by laying down his life for us (Gal.3:13). In the
passage just quoted, John 15:13-15, when one lays down his life for another, he is not treating the other as a slave but as a friend. Jesus treats
us as friends, not slaves. While it is true that we are his slaves because
Yahweh God had redeemed us with the blood of His beloved Son, that
doesn't mean that Jesus treats us merely as slaves. The next step is that
we, as his friends, are put into a special relationship with Jesus and his
Father. Everything he hears from the Father, he makes known to us.

It is possible to be a slave and a friend at the same time. In the Bible,
friendship is sometimes a deeper relationship than sonship. The
father-and-son relationship is not necessarily the closest relationship
between two persons. One can be a son yet an enemy, as in the case of
David and Absalom. At a certain point in his life, David's worst enemy
was his son Absalom who tried to take David's life as well as his kingdom. It was one of the most painful incidents in the Old Testament, so
sonship is not necessarily a good thing in itself. But when one is both a
friend and a son, that is truly beautiful.

A final question

Is it correct to say that one doesn't have to be literally poor in order to
be righteous, provided that he has the right attitude towards riches,
namely, that he acknowledges that what he has belongs to God and not
to himself? Yes, provided we are not playing games with God, saying,
"It all belongs to God" when in fact "it all belongs to me". In Scripture,
the use of one's possessions is something voluntary, for obedience is
voluntary. But if we play games with God, then we are back to a constitutional monarchy in which the Lord is not really our Lord. The

same can be said of His son: If Jesus is not our Lord, neither is he our Savior, in which case we are playing games with our eternal salvation!

But the one who is honest about God's lordship over his life and possessions will soon discover that God will instruct him on what to do with the riches. If you are ready to obey His instructions, more will come to you in a steady stream.

A closing remark: We must not recklessly throw away everything we have. We have to proceed in a scriptural manner so that all things are done properly, carefully, and according to God's will.

Chapter 5

Commitment in Practice

In the Bible, commitment has to do with practical living rather than theory. We saw this when we went through Luke's gospel to see what the Lord Jesus has to say about riches. We now look at some passages in Paul's teaching, starting with 1 Timothy 6:9-10:

> But those who want to be rich fall into temptation, a trap, and many foolish and harmful desires, which plunge people into ruin and destruction. For the love of money is a root of all kinds of evil, and by craving it, some have wandered away from the faith and pierced themselves with many pains. (1Tim.6:9-10, HCSB)

Those who love riches fall into temptation and a trap, and plunge into ruin and destruction. The love of money is a root of all sorts of evil. Money may be nothing more than paper or gold, yet the desire for it has caused many to stray from the faith, piercing themselves with many pains. Immediately before this passage, Paul says in 1Tim.6:6-8:

> But godliness with contentment is a great gain. For we brought nothing into the world, and we can take nothing out. But if we have food and clothing, we will be content with these. (HCSB)

If we have food and clothing, we ought to be content. Yet our problem is that we're never satisfied with what we've got. There is a vast difference between need and greed. What we need is far less than what our greed demands. Greed is not satisfied with any amount of money, yet what we actually need is very little. How much food do you eat daily?

You only need a small amount of food to sustain your life; greed is the part that makes life expensive and complicated.

The world feeds on greed

One day I was walking in the Tsimshatsui district of Hong Kong and walked past some stores. I couldn't believe my eyes when I saw the prices of the clothes on display. One jacket looked like it was made of ordinary cotton similar to what you can get for HK$60 (US$8) in other districts of Hong Kong, but here in Tsimshatsui, it cost over $1,000. I thought to myself, "Is this jacket sewn with gold thread?"

Another time my wife was looking for a small canvas bag. She walked into a shop, also in Tsimshatsui, thinking that the one on display might be inexpensive. When she asked about the price, the saleswoman said $1,200.

"You must be joking!"
"No, it's a designer bag made in Italy."

It was made of ordinary canvas, yet you have to pay a fortune for the luxury name. Greed is what businesses feed on.

The lottery is a lucrative business that feeds on greed. You put in a few dollars to win one million, five million, ten million. Yet it's the lottery company that makes the most money, easily hundreds of millions.

Horse racing day is a busy day in Hong Kong with traffic clogging the streets and tunnels. People bet a few dollars on a horse, hoping to win a few thousand or tens of thousands.

Greed makes us vulnerable. In reality we need very little money to survive, yet there is no limit to how much we want. Going back to the question of storing up money, exactly how much is enough? The millionaire will answer, "A little bit more, just a little bit more."

How much is enough?

It is fair to ask who is going to pay our medical bills when we get sick, or pay for our children's education or even our own education. We need money to support the family. We want to travel the world to broaden our horizons and expand our world view. On and on it goes.

Where do we draw the line? How much should we save up? That is a fair question. Does it mean that Christians cannot save up for their retirement? When they get old, who's going to feed them? Are they going to live on charity? Some countries offer social welfare, but what if you live in a country that does not?

Let's say I have $100,000 in some currency in my bank account. How do I apply Paul's teaching about being content with food and clothing? Does Scripture provide any guidance on the $100,000? The problem for us is that the New Testament views money and possessions negatively. So far we haven't seen anything in the New Testament that speaks positively of riches and money.

So what I do with the $100,000 in my account? With that amount, I would be slightly rich but not very rich. Since it is hard, even impossible, for a rich man to enter the kingdom of God, what should I do with the money? That is a very practical question. In the same chapter of First Timothy, Paul goes on to say:

> Command those who are rich in this present world not to be arrogant or put their hope in wealth, which is so uncertain, but to put their hope in God, who richly provides us with everything for our enjoyment. Command them to do good, to be rich in good deeds, and to be generous and willing to share. In this way they will lay up treasure for themselves as a firm foundation for the coming age, so that they may take hold of the life that is truly life. (1Tim.6:17-19, HCSB)

How do I apply this passage to my $100,000? I will indeed try my best not to be "arrogant" about my riches, to use Paul's word. I will be humble about the money. I will fix my hope not on the money but on God who, after all, richly supplies us with all things for our enjoyment. He is ultimately the one who gave me the $100,000 in the first place, and for that I am grateful. I am willing to do a few good works and put a few more dollars into the offering box.

Is this how we apply Paul's teaching? All this talk about generosity and good deeds sounds vague to us because we don't know how generous is generous. If we usually give $20, do we now give $100? A five-fold increase sounds generous enough, but have we fulfilled Scripture?

A sum of $100,000 may seem large but in some countries it can be wiped out by a major surgery. If I give my money to others, who will pay my medical bills? My generosity may have helped others but who will look after my medical needs? Then I will be in trouble. When I get old and sick, or need to pay for my children's education, do I trust in God to supply my need? That takes a lot of commitment!

Why can't I simply accept the $100,000 as a gift from God? After all, Paul does say that God has richly supplied us with all things for our enjoyment (1Tim.6:17), so why can't we keep it for a rainy day? If God was the one who gave me the $100,000 in the first place, why should I give it away only to seek His help again?

What about a rich church?

The people of the Jerusalem church shared all possessions in common (Acts 2:44-45; 4:32). What does that mean for me? If I join a church with a common fund that pays for everyone's needs, perhaps I won't need to save my $100,000. Then the church will take care of my needs. That seems ideal. By giving all my money to the church, it won't be stuck in a bank account but will be in circulation to meet the needs of the church people.

But the problem is that the church will get rich! Instead of the individual who stores up riches, now it is the church that stores up riches. Do we solve our problem by making the church rich? In fact a rich church will find itself in a dangerous spiritual situation. The Lord Jesus says to the church in Laodicea: "For you say, I am rich, I have prospered, and I need nothing, not realizing that you are wretched, pitiable, poor, blind, and naked" (Rev.3:17, ESV).

The danger of riches is as real to a church as to an individual, which is not surprising given that a church is composed of people. The symptoms described in this verse are true of the church and the individual alike. On the individual level, the rich Christian is wretched, miserable, poor, blind, and naked. Money can't buy happiness or the inner peace that comes from the fruit of the Spirit. These same ailments are found in the church in Laodicea. Making the church rich is not the answer to the problem of what to do with our money.[5]

The other danger of a common fund is that we will no longer put our trust in God to provide for our needs but will rely on the fund. I'm told that some become Catholic monks for this reason. After they join a monastery, the church will take care of their material needs for the rest of their lives. When they die, the church will even take care of their burial. Our faith then becomes horizontal rather than vertical.

Led by the Spirit of God

How then do we deal with the matter of money for the individual and the church? The answer comes back to Romans 8:14: "For all who are being led by the Spirit of God, these are the sons of God."

The answer is found in the leading of the Spirit. If we are willing to be led by the Spirit as a church or as individuals, God will show us what we ought to do with our money. No one can give you a specific answer to the question of what to do with your $100,000. At the most we can say that if you are a child of God, or want to be a child of God, you will have to be led by the Spirit. You will have to ask God what to do with the $100,000. No one can answer the question for you. Anyone who tells you what to do with the money is assuming an authority that he is not entitled to.

Committing to God means to be willing to be led by the Spirit in all situations. But here is a warning: If you are being led by the Spirit, you will experience an inner opposition to that leading. Galatians 5:22 talks

---

[5] Background note: The Jerusalem church was not a rich church despite its having a common fund. In fact the church was so poor that Paul had to organize a relief collection for it with contributions from the Gentile churches. The Jerusalem church had a common fund, but its limited reserves were used up when a famine struck that part of the world. It had always been poor, so much so that the Macedonian church, which was itself poor, tried its best to support the Jerusalem church. Here is a case of a poor church helping an even poorer church.

about the fruit of the Spirit, but the context also says that flesh and spirit are in conflict with each other. The unbeliever is usually unaware of this conflict because he lives as he pleases. But when you become a Christian, life suddenly gets complicated because every time you want to sin, something comes along and fights your impulses. Every time you have a sinful thought, another thought comes in and starts fighting it. You feel that you are being pulled apart.

The Christian life will be extremely difficult if you allow the flesh—that is, your old way of thinking, your old habits, your old nature—to exert its control in your life, because the Holy Spirit will not tolerate that. This will lead to an inner conflict in which the flesh pulls you in one direction and the Spirit in the other. To be led by the Spirit without conflict, you must put off the old nature.

But when you are being led by the Spirit, every experience from God will bear His mark so that you will know it is from God. Your experience of God will be as real as your experience of sin. After you sin, you immediately become aware that you have sinned. Similarly, when you are being led by the Spirit, you are aware of the leading, for there is a self-confirming aspect to it.

A new heart, a new spirit

Yahweh God says in Ezekiel 36:26-27:

> I will give you a new heart and put a new spirit within you; I will remove your heart of stone and give you a heart of flesh. I will place My Spirit within you and cause you to follow My statutes and carefully observe My ordinances. (HCSB)

In Scripture, the word "flesh" usually has a negative meaning but here it is given a positive meaning as a contrast to the coldness of stone. It is important, however, to keep in mind that the word "flesh" outside this passage usually has a negative meaning.

What is the difference between a heart of stone and a heart of flesh? We are not talking about a physical heart but about sensitivity to God. Whereas stone is cold and insensitive, flesh is sensitive to touch, to pain, to temperature. To be led by the Spirit means to be sensitive to

God. Many Christians are not being led because they are not spiritually sensitive, having a heart of stone rather than a heart of flesh. God cannot speak to them because their hearts don't respond to Him. But when we receive His Spirit, He will give us a new heart and a new life. When you are sensitive to the Spirit's leading, you will be surprised at how much God is willing to lead you.

How am I going to be led by the Spirit? What must I do on my part? At the very least, I must be willing to be led. But is willingness enough? Your willingness will be tested when the Spirit brings about changes in your life, and you struggle over whether to follow the leading. You may be able to endure this kind of struggle for a short time, but can you carry on like this in the long stretch? When difficulties or pressures arise, will your willingness rise to the challenge? What will you do when you face the ultimate test and your life is at stake? Martyrdom sounds grand, and some hope to experience it one day, but most Christians don't welcome martyrdom.

In real life, the things that hinder Christians from following the Spirit's leading are usually the tiny problems that chip away at their willingness. It is the sniper fire rather than the artillery fire that wears down many a soldier and makes him a nervous wreck. It is the slow chiseling that gradually causes the whole structure to collapse. When Christians collapse, in most cases it is not because of a great calamity but the slow chipping away at their commitment.

Sonship and slavery

But the one who is willing to be led unconditionally by the Spirit is committed to God. The word "unconditionally" is important because slaves don't lay down conditions. But you may ask: Isn't all this teaching about slavery negated by the fact that we are sons of God?

I will preface my answer to this question with a statement I will prove shortly from Scripture: In scriptural teaching, the question is not whether you choose to be a slave or a son. The fact is that you are a son only if you are a slave. If you are not a slave, you are not a son. In other words, being a son and being a slave are not two separate things in

Scripture but two pictures of the same thing. If you are a slave, you are a son, and vice versa.

The first evidence for this comes from Romans 6 which says we have been set free from slavery to sin and have become slaves of God. You are the one or the other, either a slave of sin or a slave of God, with no middle ground between them. No one in the world is truly free in the absolute sense because you are a slave to something, either to sin or to God. Yet on the other hand, we can say that it is the slaves of God who are free in a real and experiential sense because they are also the sons of God. Whereas Romans 6 speaks of our being slaves of God, Romans 8 speaks of our being sons of God (notably 8:14 regarding the leading of the Spirit). The slaves of God in Romans 6 are the sons of God in Romans 8.

Secondly, in the Bible, son and slave are two aspects of the same thing. You cannot be the one without being the other. The New Testament's definition of sonship is different from the human concept of it. The Bible defines a son as one who is obedient to God and His will. We see this in Mt.12:50 (and its parallels in Mk.3:35 and Lk.8:21): "For whoever does the will of my Father in heaven is my brother and sister and mother."

Jesus is the Son of God, so anyone who is a brother of Jesus is also a son of God (a common title of Christians, Mt.5:9; Rom.8:14; Gal.3:26). And who is Jesus' brother and therefore God's son? The one who does the will of the Father in heaven. In a parallel, Luke 8:21, Jesus says, "My mother and my brothers are those who hear the word of God and do it". Hence a son of God is one who obeys God's will and God's word unconditionally. This unique definition of sonship is equally applicable to a slave of God, for a slave likewise obeys his master's will unconditionally. From all this, we see that being a son and being a slave amount to the same thing for the Christian. Jesus says to his disciples:

> [15] If you love me, you will keep my commandments. [16] And I will ask the Father, and he will give you another Helper, to be with you forever, [17] even the Spirit of truth, whom the world cannot receive, because it neither sees him nor knows him. You know him, for he dwells with you and will be in you. (John 14:15-17, ESV)

Whether you call yourself a son or a slave is not the issue; ultimately it is whether you keep God's commandments (v.15). This applies to son and slave in the same way. The distinction between son and slave is one of terminology. In practice they are the same since both are committed to keeping God's commandments and doing His will.

The third line of evidence for the functional equivalence of son and slave is the work of the Spirit. The one who keeps God's commandments is given the Holy Spirit (Acts 5:32) who is the Helper and the Spirit of truth (John 14:16-17, just quoted). On the other hand, John 1:12 says, "Yet to all who received him, to those who believed in his name, he gave the right to become children of God." What is this right? Why does John bring in the idea of right? It refers to the Holy Spirit. To receive this right is to receive the Spirit. It is also the right to become sons of God, for the sons of God are those who are being led by the Spirit (Rom.8:14), having "received the Spirit of adoption as sons" (v.15).

If you have not received the Spirit or are not being led by the Spirit, you are not a son of God, not even if you have been baptized. The Spirit is the key to the Christian life. There is no Christian life without the Spirit. In receiving the Spirit, you are given the right to be a son of God. With that right comes the responsibility of being led by the Spirit every moment. If you are a Christian, are you willing to let the Spirit lead you in practical ways such as: What shall I do with the money in my bank account? What should I do about my past sins? How do I resolve my relationship problems with the church brothers and sisters? The Spirit's leading has to do with everyday practical living.

First link: To believe is to follow

We have seen in John 1:12 that to receive God is to believe in Him, and the same could be said of His Son Jesus Christ, the one sent by the Father (John 6:38,39,44; 7:16,28,33). If to receive is to believe, then to believe is to follow, as seen by comparing the following two statements:

I have come into the world as a light, so that no one who *believes* in me should stay in darkness. (John 12:46, NIV)

I am the light of the world. Whoever *follows* me will never walk in darkness, but will have the light of life. (John 8:12, NIV)

Both verses speak of turning away from darkness. The first verse links this to believing in Jesus, the second to following Jesus. Together they show the functional equivalence of "believe" and "follow," a connection seen also in John 10:26-27: "you do not *believe* because you are not my sheep. My sheep listen to my voice; I know them, and they *follow* me."

Second link: To follow is to serve

We come to the next functional link: To follow Jesus is to serve him. "Whoever *serves* me must *follow* me; and where I am, my servant also will be. My Father will honor the one who *serves* me." (Jn.12:26, NIV)

Here the Greek word for "serve" (*diakoneō*) is related to the one from which we get the English word "deacon". It is different from the word for serving as a slave. However, in the New Testament, there is little practical difference between the two. On the one hand, Jesus says, "I am among you as the one who serves" (Lk.22:27), using the word from which *deacon* is derived. On the other hand, Jesus took on "the form of a slave" (Phil. 2:7). Hence *serve* and *slave* are applied to him with almost no functional difference in meaning.

Third link: To serve is to die

Now comes the hard part about commitment: to serve is to die. If you are at all serious about committing to God and following the Spirit's leading, you will have to know where the Lord will lead you: *to the cross*. "If anyone would come after me, he must deny himself and take up his cross and follow me." (Mt.16:24)

We have seen that the Spirit is the key to the Christian life; without the Spirit there is no Christian life. A related principle is that *spiritual life comes through death.* This principle, that there is no life without death, is seen in several New Testament passages, for example:

> [23] And Jesus answered them, "The hour has come for the Son of Man to be glorified. [24] Truly, truly, I say to you, unless a grain of wheat falls into the earth and dies, it remains alone; but if it dies, it bears much fruit. [25] Whoever loves his life loses it, and whoever hates his life in this world will keep it for eternal life." (John 12:23-25, ESV)

Hating one's life in the world may seem radical but it is the path to spiritual fruitfulness (v.24). A grain of wheat remains a lone grain that accomplishes nothing until it falls into the earth and dies. How does one grain become many? How does it pass on life? By being buried into the earth. Then emerges a stalk that will later have many grains on it. One grain of wheat becomes many grains, for life and fruitfulness come from death.

And who attains to eternal life? Read this verse carefully and don't let any false teacher sidetrack you with a teaching of cheap grace. Jesus says, "Whoever hates his life in this world will keep it for eternal life". To keep your life for eternity, you must hate your life in this world.

What does it mean to hate your life? Some willingly die in service for their country; they consider their country as being more important than their own lives. They "hate" their lives in the sense that they value something above their own lives.

Conversely, you won't surrender your physical life unless you see eternal life as being of greater value than your physical life. It takes total commitment to hate your life, to deny your life. There is no higher commitment than that.

The word "hate" conveys intensity. Hating one's life is not the same as a passive surrender to death. If you are dying from a terminal illness, it won't make any difference whether you hate your life or not. It is meaningless to talk about hating your life when it's about to end. But while you're still in reasonably good health, you have the opportunity to make a meaningful decision to hate your own life.

In terms of conceptual flow, it is significant that verse 24 is a bridge between verse 23 and verse 25. Verse 23 says that the Son of Man is about to be "glorified," which in John's gospel means that Jesus is about to be crucified. That is why Jesus speaks of himself as being "lifted up" (v.32), a play on words that has dual meaning: glorification and crucifixion. The upward action in "lifted up" expresses glorification but also crucifixion, for the cross is literally lifted up at crucifixion. Jesus' death is his glorification whereas the world sees crucifixion as the ultimate humiliation; in fact he was crucified between two robbers. But in spiritual thinking, what is humiliation in the eyes of the world is glorification in Christ.

Whereas verse 23 refers to Jesus, verse 25 refers to us. The picture of the grain of wheat (v.24) is sandwiched in between the two verses. Hence it applies to Jesus and to us, bringing out a beautiful picture of the spiritual life. Here we see Christ's absolute commitment to us. By his death as a grain of wheat, he passed on his life to you and me. His death gives us life. One life has multiplied into many. But the Lord doesn't let the process stop there. The farmer keeps a small portion of the harvest for the next sowing, to obtain yet another harvest. Year after year there will be new harvests. The way to benefit from the life Jesus passes to us is not to keep it to ourselves, but to let it fall into the ground and die, in order to pass on life to others.

A vital attribute of life is the capacity to pass on life. Romans 4:19 notes the "deadness" of Sarah's womb while Abraham's body was "as good as dead" in terms of their ability to have children. Dead means to be unable to produce life. But those who have life can pass on life. Commitment means to live the kind of life Jesus lived. As he passed on his life to us, so we pass on life to others. This is the kind of person who will have eternal life.

Chapter 6

The Abundant Christian Life

How many of us know what is the abundant Christian life? If you have never experienced it, you wouldn't be able to imagine what it is like just as you wouldn't know what Canada or Europe is like if you haven't visited those places. How would you explain what is the abundant Christian life to those who haven't experienced it?

If you see nothing attractive about the Christian life, is there anything that will motivate you to seek after it? Perhaps what is driving you forward is the realization that the life you now have is empty and devoid of joy and meaning. Perhaps you feel that this kind of life is not worth continuing in, so you want to move on to something better.

If I were promoting Canada, I might show you posters of Canada's forests, rivers, parks, and the Rocky Mountains. Then you can look at the posters and say, "So this is Canada!" But I can't show you photos of the abundant Christian life in the way I show you photos of Canada or the beautiful Swiss Alps. So how can you visualize the spiritual life?

One way is to get to know a few people of God, to see the quality of their lives. As a young Christian in China, I had the privilege of knowing one or two men of God. I lived with them, got to know them, and saw them in action. You need to see them in action in the field, not just in a teaching environment. Then you will see what a soldier is made of, not when he is marching in a parade, but in combat. Then you will see his military experience and combat skills. But you won't see any of this just by sitting in front of him and listening to a lecture on military tactics.

Is there anything in the spiritual life that speaks to your heart? When you listen to testimonies, you marvel at the spiritual experiences of those who walk with God. Because these experiences are second-hand to you, you might say to yourself, "These experiences are real for him but not for me." But the point of a testimony is that it can be real for you too, even in the matter of being led by the Spirit. The leading of the Spirit will be just theory to you until you experience it in real life.

And where do you see this kind of dynamic life today? The sad reality is that very few in the world live a victorious and dynamic life. The Bible has already warned us that there will be few:

> Enter by the narrow gate. For the gate is wide and the way is easy that leads to destruction, and those who enter by it are many. For the gate is narrow and the way is hard that leads to life, and those who find it are few. (Matthew 7:13-14, ESV)

The ongoing challenge that we face in the Christian life is that there is always an easy road in front of us to tempt us. Most of us will go for the easy road, a few will take the narrow road. Why so few? After all, there are two billion Christians in the world today: over a billion Catholics plus several hundred million Protestants plus several hundred million from the Orthodox churches. The statistics are impressive, yet "few" will find the narrow gate that leads to life.

Will you find the narrow gate? Will Jesus' words in John 10:10 be fulfilled in you: "I came that they may have life and have it abundantly"? Jesus is talking about the present life, not the future. He wants you to live the fullness of the abundant life right now.

What will a man give in exchange for his soul?

When the Christian life gets tough, you may wonder if it's worth it. Jesus brings out this issue when he says, "What will a man give in exchange for his soul?" (Mt.16:26). Is your financial wealth too valuable to exchange for your soul? What will you give in exchange for eternal life? Matthew 10:39 goes straight to the issue: "Whoever finds his life will lose it, but whoever loses his life for my sake will find it." If you find your life in the world, you will lose it. But if you lose your life for Jesus' sake, you will find it. This is also brought out in Mt.16:25-26:

> For whoever wants to save his life will lose it, but whoever loses his life for me will find it. What good will it be for a man if he gains the whole world, yet forfeits his soul? Or what can a man give in exchange for his soul? (NIV)

We are selfish by nature and it is mainly because of our selfishness that we are sinful. The Lord Jesus seeks to change the direction of our lives from a selfish way of thinking to a self-giving one. To effect this change in our lives, he attaches a condition to eternal life.

The words "love" and "hate" convey strong attitudes (as in loving your life versus hating your life, Jn.12:25). If you love your life, you are walking on the broad road to destruction. If you hate your life, you will save it to life eternal. When the Bible says to hate your life, it doesn't mean to hate the life you have in Christ, but the life that is in bondage to sin. To break free from this bondage, all you do on your part is to kneel before God and say, "Dear God, I hate the life I have been living, seeking praise from men among other things. I ask you to change my life." We do our part and God does the rest. The Holy Spirit comes in, and you will experience God's power.

Many Christians live in selfishness because they have been taught that they only need to "believe" to gain eternal life, even if there is no fundamental change in their lives. But this is not biblical teaching. In the last chapter we saw that to believe in the biblical sense means to follow, which means to serve, which means to die. You have to lose your life for Christ's sake before you can receive eternal life. You have to change from a selfish way of living to one that is self-giving.

I am not playing around with words. On judgment day when you and I stand before God, if you lose your life and are condemned to eternal destruction, let it not be said that I didn't make this truth clear to you. Paul says to the Ephesians, "I testify to you this day that I am innocent of everyone's blood, for I did not shrink back from declaring to you the whole plan of God" (Acts 20:26-27, HCSB). I am telling you from God's word that you must change from a self-centered life to a self-giving one, by the power of the Holy Spirit.

We don't have the power to transform ourselves because we cannot save ourselves. Salvation is entirely of grace because it is attained only by God's power. We cannot change ourselves any more than a leopard can change its spots (Jer.13:23).

Since this is achieved by the Spirit's work in us, all we can do on our part is to be willing to be changed. Are we willing to let the Spirit change us? If a sick person refuses medical treatment, the doctor won't go to his house and drag him to hospital. Likewise God won't drag you kicking and screaming into the kingdom of God. You have to tell God whether you want eternal life or not.

What must I do to be saved?

False teaching is often presented as the truth, and many cannot tell the difference. An example is the way we water down Paul's statement, "Believe in the Lord Jesus and you will be saved" (Acts 16:31). This comes from a well known incident in Acts 16.

In the city of Philippi, Paul and Silas were beaten by the local authorities and thrown in jail on false charges. In jail they began to sing songs of praise to God. That makes them a bit odd, doesn't it? Yet the odd thing about people filled with the Spirit is that they sing praises to God even after they have been beaten black and blue and thrown in jail. Paul and Silas were so badly injured that their wounds had to be attended to later. Yet they weren't thinking about nursing their injuries or easing the pain, but were rejoicing and singing praises to God. That is the victorious and abundant life.

A powerful earthquake ripped through the prison. The walls crumbled, the gates fell, and everything was breaking into pieces. The jailer thought that the prisoners had escaped, Paul and Silas among them.

The city of Philippi was a Roman colony, so the jailer was probably a Roman soldier, either active or retired. After supposing that the prisoners had escaped, he knew what punishment was waiting for him: beheading. Roman military code was severe and merciless. The jailer wanted to spare himself the dishonor of a military trial, so he got ready to commit suicide: "The jailer woke up, and when he saw the prison doors open, he drew his sword and was about to kill himself because he thought the prisoners had escaped." (Acts 16:27, NIV)

If the jailer had killed himself, you could imagine what would have happened to his wife and children, his "household". In Roman society, when a man died, his wife would be unable to support herself, much less her family, unlike today's career women with college degrees. When a man died, his wife would be in a pitiful, even tragic situation. A family's dependence on the head of the household was almost total. That is why when the head of a household comes to the Lord, the household would usually follow.

Paul's statement, "believe in the Lord Jesus and you will be saved," was spoken to a man who was ready to die. When you quote that to someone, is that person ready to die as was the Philippian jailer? If so, then you can tell him or her, "Believe in the Lord Jesus and you will be saved," since the part about dying has been dealt with. But if you leave out the element of death, Paul's statement would be taken in the wrong way.

Paul's teaching about baptism

Paul cried out to the jailer, imploring him not to kill himself. The jailer in turn pleaded, "What must I do to be saved?" to which Paul replied, "Believe in the Lord Jesus and you will be saved" (Acts 16:30-31). But that is not the end of the story. Paul didn't say, "Believe and you will be saved. Now sign your name on the baptismal form." Verse 32 tells us what happened next: "They spoke the word of the Lord to him together with all who were in his house." This was in preparation for their baptism.

Paul and Silas were giving them solid teaching from "the word of the Lord" on what it means to believe in Jesus. Paul was thorough in everything he did, and he did not jump to baptism immediately. The baptism would come only after he had given them instruction from the word of God. Because of Paul's thoroughness in God's word, the jailer and his family could easily have received a few hours of solid instruction. Only afterwards came the baptism.

In all this time, Paul's wounds were still untreated, perhaps still bleeding. It was only after the teaching had finished that Paul and Silas allowed the jailer to treat their wounds. Paul had his priorities: first the teaching of salvation, then the treating of his wounds. Saving others was more important than his own physical welfare. When we read the Bible attentively, we catch small details that reveal important things, in this case the life quality of Paul and Silas. We miss these vital details when we read the Bible hastily or superficially.

Baptism and death to sin

So what did Paul teach the jailer and his household? We can be sure that he would not teach them anything contrary to what he has written in his letters. We have enough of Paul's letters to have a good idea of what he taught them: *Before baptizing them, Paul simply taught what he himself taught about baptism in his letters, and what Jesus himself taught.* Many Christians think that Paul taught differently from the Lord Jesus, e.g. that whereas Jesus told us to hate our lives in order to gain eternal life, Paul made things easy for us by saying that we only need to believe in Jesus. But Acts 16:31 ("believe in the Lord Jesus and you will be saved") has to be understood in the light of Paul's whole teaching.

Paul, like Jesus, taught emphatically that there is no life without death. Romans 6, which talks about baptism, gives us a good idea of what Paul might have told the Philippian jailer before baptizing him. In Romans 6, Paul explicitly links baptism and death:

> Shall we go on sinning so that grace may increase? By no means! We died to sin; how can we live in it any longer? Or don't you know that all of us who were baptized into Christ Jesus were *baptized into his death?* (Romans 6:1-3, NIV)

We can be sure that when Paul was about to baptize the jailer, he had already explained to him the meaning of baptism. In Romans 6 he says that baptism involves death. Does he mean this in some fictional or metaphorical sense? Is baptism a pretend death? Or do we die to sin in some real sense?

Paul is not so superficial as to play around with weighty words and then arrive at superficial meanings. "Die" is not a word to play around with. If "die to sin" means nothing more than "forget about sin," then we must not use the word "die". But Paul does use the word "die," so it must mean something weighty.

What does it mean to die to sin? Is it a change of attitude? And does a mere change of attitude deserve to be described by a weighty word such as "die" or "death"? If an evil person wants to implement some reform in his lifestyle, can that change be properly described as death?

To be sure, a change of attitude is an important first step towards the death that Paul talks about. But is it the same as death? Is "death to sin" just a change of attitude, or is it something deeper?

The word "sin" in the singular doesn't refer to specific deeds of sin but to the whole way of life dominated by sin. Therefore "death to sin" means a complete break from the old way of life. If I am finished with my old way of life, I have died to it.

Death is more than reform; it is something deep that the Holy Spirit does in us. I can achieve moral reform without God's help, but when Paul talks about death, he does not mean moral reform. He is speaking of something that the Spirit does in us so deep and decisive that something in us has died. That part of us which is controlled by the flesh and is responsive to the flesh—which Paul elsewhere calls the "old man"—has been put to death by the work of the Spirit.

Moral reform requires some measure of commitment but not of the kind the Bible talks about. Being a Christian is not a matter of moral reform but the commitment to let the Spirit put to death the "old man" in us. Everyone accepts reform to one degree or another, especially after seeing the ugliness of bad and the beauty of good. But that is not what being a Christian is about. Mere reform is like patching an old garment with new cloth, or pouring new wine into an old wineskin, an act that will ruin wine and wineskin (Mt.9:16-17).

But the Spirit works deep to destroy the cancer of sin in us. This is accomplished by God, not moral reform. Salvation is entirely of grace because it is achieved solely by God's power.

In the New Testament, our commitment to God is *faith*, God's commitment to us is *grace*. We are saved by grace through faith, that is, by God's commitment to us working through our commitment to God. Salvation is ultimately by God's grace, without which we would be left with only moral reform.

We can now hear what Paul told the Philippian jailer: "Killing yourself will accomplish nothing, so let the Spirit of God destroy the disease of sin in you and bring God's life into your life by your death to sin."

Freed from slavery

Romans chapter 6 takes about death, but the second half of the chapter draws a contrast between slavery to sin and slavery to righteousness:

> But thanks be to God that, though you used to be *slaves to sin*, you wholeheartedly obeyed the form of teaching to which you were entrusted. You have been set free from sin and have become *slaves to righteousness*. (Romans 6:17-18, NIV)

We previously mentioned three ways in which a person can become a slave. There are similarly three ways one can be freed from slavery.

The first way to be freed from slavery is by the death of the slave.

The second way is for your master to release you voluntarily. But if your master happens to be sin which enslaved you in the first place, you can rule out any voluntary surrender of the slave into the hands of Christ. Hence death still remains the way for us to be freed from slavery to sin. If our death is not real, neither is our so-called freedom. A slave doesn't cease to be a slave just by playing dead. His pretending to be a corpse won't fool anyone. Unless there is true death, there is no true release from slavery. Through death we are freed from slavery to sin, "for he who has died is freed from sin" (Rom.6:7).

The third way to be freed from slavery is by *redemption*: the paying of a ransom to release a slave from slavery. It is significant that Christ's redemptive death for us is tied to our death with him.

Christ died for us, and we die with him in baptism. Romans 6 has many references to our death in baptism (see the underlined), showing beyond any doubt that baptism involves death:

> ³ Do you not know that all of us who have been baptized into Christ Jesus were baptized into his death? ⁴ We were buried therefore with him by baptism into death, in order that, just as Christ was raised from the dead by the glory of the Father, we too might walk in newness of life. ⁵ For if we have been united with him in a death like his, we shall certainly be united with him in a resurrection like his. ⁶ We know that our old self was crucified with him in order that the body of sin might be brought to nothing, so that we would no longer be enslaved to sin. ⁷ For one who has died has been set free from sin. ⁸ Now if we have died with Christ, we believe that we will also live with him. (Romans 6:3-8, ESV)

The theme of the next chapter, Romans 7, is the Law. Our bondage to sin is compounded by our bondage to the Law, and the same question arises: How can I be set free from the Law? Or from the power of sin? Or from the guilt of sin, since the Law condemns me? The answer in Romans 7 is the same: *death*. Through death we are freed from the Law and from guilt, as seen especially in verses 1 to 4.

In the next chapter, Romans 8, Paul continues on the topic of death yet he also speaks of victory in the Spirit: "For if you live according to the flesh you will die, but if by the Spirit you put to death the deeds of the body, you will live." (Rom.8:13) This reminds us of John 12:24 and Matthew 10 and 16, demonstrating that Paul's teachings are undergirded by Jesus' teachings. Paul does not alter or diverge from Jesus' teaching, but teaches the same.

The next verse, Romans 8:14, regarding the leading of the Spirit, has already been discussed. This verse begins with the word "for", indicating a logical connection between verses 13 and 14:

[13] For if you live according to the flesh you will die, but if by the Spirit you put to death the deeds of the body, you will live. [14] For all who are led by the Spirit of God are sons of God. (Rom.8:13-14, ESV)

We won't be led by the Spirit unless we allow the Spirit to "put to death" the deeds of the flesh. If we skip the part about putting to death the deeds of the flesh, and try to go straight to the wonderful life of being led by the Spirit—even experiencing an earthquake from God— we are going to be disappointed. The wonderful life in the Spirit comes only after the Spirit has put to death the flesh in us. First death, then life, in that order.

The deeds of the flesh

What then are the deeds of the flesh? Paul tells us:

> Now the works of the flesh are evident: sexual immorality, impurity, sensuality, idolatry, sorcery, enmity, strife, jealousy, fits of anger, rivalries, dissensions, divisions, envy, drunkenness, orgies, and things like these. I warn you, as I warned you before, that those who do such things will not inherit the kingdom of God. (Gal.5:19-21, ESV)

Those who do the deeds of the flesh won't inherit the kingdom of God. You might say that you don't do most of these things. But it takes only one deed to be guilty of all, just as you need only break one commandment to be guilty of breaking the whole law (James 2:10; Gal.5:3). Sorcery or drunkenness might not apply to you but what about jealousy or fits of anger? How many of us can go through this list and come away with a clean sheet?

Paul is not talking to unbelievers but Galatian believers. He tells them that if they do the deeds of the flesh, they won't inherit the kingdom of God even if they claim to believe in Jesus. But in contrast to the deeds of the flesh, the abundant life is characterized by the fruit of the Spirit: "But the fruit of the Spirit is love, joy, peace, patience, kindness, goodness, faithfulness, gentleness and self-control. Against such things there is no law." (Gal.5:22-23)

Die to the world

Finally, we die not only to sin but to the world: "May I never boast except in the cross of our Lord Jesus Christ, through which the world has been crucified to me, and I to the world." (Gal.6:14)

If we are united with Christ, we are also crucified to the world. We are dead to the world and the world is dead to us. If you have died with Christ and if the cross avails for your salvation, then through the cross you are dead to the world, and the world to you.

Here "the world" does not refer to lakes, trees, mountains, birds. We don't die to these things. In fact these become more meaningful to us than ever before, for now we see in them God's glory. In the Bible, "the world" refers to the world system enslaved to sin. The whole world lies in the power of Satan, the evil one (1Jn.5:19). If we have died to sin, we have also died to the world. We have been set free from the values of the world and the way of thinking dominated by sin.

We live in a sordid world. The higher up you are in the world, the fiercer is the battle and the more sinister the tactics of your rivals. But when you are in the lower ranks, no one is interested in you, a nobody.

A good friend of mine in the Japanese Foreign Ministry has twice written me pleading for prayer support. He was due to be transferred to Africa as a discipline for a deed he had not committed. He was a victim of a conspiracy in the foreign office where he worked. He was due to become the ambassador of a certain country in his next posting, but someone coveted that position.

Every country has a limited number of ambassadors, perhaps 100 to 150. The ambassadorial positions are not of equal rank or prestige. The ambassador to a country such as the United States enjoys greater prestige. At the bottom ranks are the ambassadors to countries which you have trouble finding on a map. An ambassador is still an ambassador, but some are "more equal" than others in the real world.

There was infighting for the ambassadorial position that was to be my friend's. The tactic was simple: take the job away from him by slandering him. Tell the boss that he had done this and that, and if the boss believes you, your target will be demoted or reassigned. That was what happened to my friend, so he was reassigned to Tanzania. He could have been the ambassador to France, regarded as being of higher standing than an ambassador to Tanzania. My friend wasn't concerned about the prestige because he doesn't despise any country, including Tanzania. The problem was that his wife, being in poor health, would not be able to go with him to Tanzania because the climate there was unsuitable for her health. Hence, during his posting in Tanzania, he was separated from his family. Because his sick wife was going through hardship, the whole affair was causing him a lot of grief.

That is how things are in the world. When the Bible says we are to die to the world, it means to die to this way of doing things and stepping on others. Without death, there is no entering into life. This death is a real death effected in us by the Holy Spirit, who then leads us into the fullness of life.

Chapter 7

Commitment and Compassion, Good and Evil

Do not be yoked with unbelievers

The path to life is a hard road and a narrow gate. That is why some Christians do things that are a compromise between the Christian life and life in the world. But compromise is ultimately self-deception, and was already a problem in the churches that Paul had built up by God's grace. And because compromise has serious spiritual consequences, Paul gives us an exhortation on dealing with unbelievers:

> Do not be yoked together with unbelievers. For what do righteousness and wickedness have in common? Or what fellowship can light have with darkness? What harmony is there between Christ and Belial? What does a believer have in common with an unbeliever? What agreement is there between the temple of God and idols? For we are the temple of the living God. As God has said: "I will live with them and walk among them, and I will be their God, and they will be my people." "Therefore come out from them and be separate, says the Lord. Touch no unclean thing, and I will receive you." "I will be a Father to you, and you will be my sons and daughters, says the Lord Almighty." (2Cor.6:14-18, NIV)

The term "yoked together" ("bound together" in some Bibles) can be understood in various ways. This passage is often taken as a reference to marriage, in which case Paul would be telling the Christians not to marry non-Christians. But more generally it refers to any kind of binding relationship between believers and unbelievers, whether it is a business partnership or a legal covenant, of which marriage is an example. Paul says there is no common ground between believers and unbelievers, yet many Christians see much common ground.

What does it mean to be yoked together? Does it mean to establish a legal contract? Or a friendship? Can we say that marriage is a binding relationship but friendship is not? Some Christians have been ruined by their friendship with non-Christians, so does it mean that we may not be friends with non-Christians? We can narrow the question and ask at what point a friendship ceases to be an ordinary friendship and becomes a bond. Do we regard our office coworkers as mere colleagues and not as friends? In fact James says that friendship with the world is an adulterous bond:

> You adulterous people, don't you know that friendship with the world is hatred toward God? Anyone who chooses to be a friend of the world becomes an enemy of God. (James 4:4, NIV)

If we are friends with the world, we become enemies of God according to James who doesn't seem to offer a middle ground for being friends with both. Are we then to distance ourselves from non-Christians? Few people actually think so, but wouldn't that run into a problem with James 4:4, which says that we are now thereby enemies of God?

Jesus, a friend of sinners

Yet Jesus was a friend of tax collectors and "sinners" (Mt.11:19; Lk.7:34). The word "sinners" often refers to people such as prostitutes. Tax collectors and prostitutes were the outcasts of Jewish society. Jesus was accused of being a friend to these people who were viewed by society as morally contemptible.

That creates a dilemma. Why is it okay for us to be friends with sinners but not with the world? James 4:4 clearly says that friendship with the world is enmity towards God, yet Jesus was a friend of sinners. Is there a difference between friendship with sinners and friendship with the world?

The key difference, of course, lies in one's motives. Being friends with the world in the sense of James 4:4 means gaining the world for one's own benefit. The motive is entirely selfish for it seeks after riches, position and glory in the world even at the cost of one's own soul. But when Jesus befriended sinners, his motive was to bring salvation to tax collectors and sinners—at the cost of his own life. That is the key difference between the two types of friendship.

We are to be friends with the people of the world with the aim of showing them God's love so that they may be saved. We show love and friendship to non-Christians even if they are not our family members, just as we love our family members even if they are not Christians. We give ourselves and our hearts to them in order to win them to God and not to ourselves, that they may be freed from sin and have eternal life. At school or work, our friendship with our classmates and colleagues ought to be motivated by a self-giving love that channels God's saving love to them.

In all this, there must be no ulterior selfishness. Boy-girl relationships are complicated because they often involve conflicting motives. You want to win someone to God, yet you also want to win him or her to yourself. You may even try to win the person to God in order to have him or her to yourself.

Where there are conflicting motives, the one that usually dominates is the selfish one. It is best to find someone with no ulterior motives to help him or her, or what may happen is that the one you are trying to help may become a Christian just to please you. You would have done the person a great disservice by encouraging him or her to become a Christian without committing to God. We don't become true Christians except by committing to God in response to His commitment to us. We love God because He first loved us.

Love calls for a commitment that gives of oneself without selfish motives. But where there is carnal friendship and spiritual friendship, these will cancel each other, or will be in conflict until one of them—usually the carnal one—dominates.

Why do we commit in the first place?

So far we have looked at God's commitment to us. But in the Sermon on the Mount, we also see Jesus' commitment to us. It is an expression of his brotherly love for us, for Jesus is our brother (Mt.28:10; Rom. 8:29; Heb.2:11). He was born of God just as we are born of God (1Jn. 5:18), and he cares about even the least of his brethren (Mt.25:40). Let us now consider what he says in Matthew 5:38-41:

> You have heard that it was said, An eye for an eye and a tooth for a tooth. But I tell you, don't resist an evildoer. On the contrary, if anyone slaps you on your right cheek, turn the other to him also. As for the one who wants to sue you and take away your shirt, let him have your coat as well. And if anyone forces you to go one mile, go with him two. (Mt.5:38-41, HCSB)

Many find this statement difficult. To appreciate what it means for us, it would be helpful to keep in mind that it was powerfully fulfilled in Jesus' own life by his commitment to us. Did Jesus himself fulfill these words? If he had not, he could hardly expect us to fulfill them.

Here we address a question that is in the minds of many Christians: Why should we be committed to God in the first place? Is it just to be saved? Or are there deeper reasons for commitment? Do we commit to God in blind obedience, not understanding the reasons for our commitment?

These questions are relevant to the passage we have just read. Do I turn the other cheek in blind obedience to the Lord's command? Some may put it this way: "Turning the cheek makes no sense to me, but I'll do it just the same because Jesus said so. Even if I don't like it, I'll do it to be saved. Jesus did say in John 15:14, 'You are my friends if you do what I command you'. Since he commanded me to turn the other cheek, I will turn the other cheek in order to be saved."

If you're a Christian, do you know why you're a Christian? Or why you're walking on the narrow road? If the best answer you can give is to be saved, that is not a good answer. It is not a wrong answer either, but surely there must be a better answer. It is fine to want to be saved, but you need to know why you're a Christian beyond wanting to be saved.

Why do I turn the other cheek? If someone wants my shirt, why do I give him my coat as well? And where do we see this kind of Christianity being practiced in the world today? If "believing" in Jesus is good enough for the Christian life, why do we need the Sermon on the Mount or the rest of the Bible? If commitment makes no difference for salvation, why don't we just select a few verses on believing in Jesus and forget the rest of the Bible?

Merely believing that Jesus died for my sins requires no commitment on my part, but turning the other cheek takes total commitment. The commitment has to be total because partial commitment is compromise. But is compromise even possible in the case of turning the cheek? You do it or you don't. You go a second mile or you don't.

We are confronted with two questions. First, do we need to be committed to be saved? Second, why does the Lord require commitment from us? These are vital questions that we need to answer. Pertinent to the first question is what Jesus says at the end of the Sermon on the Mount:

> And everyone who hears these words of mine and does not do them will be like a foolish man who built his house on the sand. And the rain fell, and the floods came, and the winds blew and beat against that house, and it fell, and great was the fall of it. (Mt.7:26-27, ESV)

The one who hears Jesus' words but doesn't do them is like a man who builds a house on sand. Its structure won't survive the flood of judgment. But the one who hears Jesus' words and does them is like a man who builds a house on solid rock. When the floods and storms of judgment come, it survives triumphantly. Will our lives survive the test of judgment?

Compassion: the motivation of commitment

To see the true meaning of turning the other cheek, we need to understand the motivation of commitment as we see it in the heart of Jesus. Throughout the gospels, everything he did was a fulfillment of what he had taught his disciples. His whole life displayed his total commitment to us. The Sermon on the Mount ends in chapter 7, and straightaway in chapter 8, Jesus cleanses a leper.

When I first arrived in Hong Kong, I visited a leper colony there. It was quite an experience for me to see people disfigured by a hideous disease, with limbs contorted and parts falling off.

The leper symbolizes mankind in its sinful condition. There is nothing healthy about the sinner from the top of his head to the soles of his feet. The whole person is corrupted by sin. It is no coincidence that right after giving the Sermon on the Mount, the first thing Jesus did was to cleanse a leper. The word *cleanse* means to heal or to restore to good condition. After cleansing the leper, the next thing Jesus did was to heal a centurion's servant.

We often miss the point of Jesus' miracles. They are not meant to showcase his wonder-working powers. In fact Jesus would often tell the healed person not to tell anyone about the healing (Mt.8:4; Mk. 7:36; 8:26; Lk.8:56). He wasn't trying to impress anyone with his healing powers. On the contrary, every miracle is a sign that points to the fact that Jesus, out of his deep compassion, has come to heal and save us.

Compassion in Matthew's gospel

Since it was compassion that motivated Jesus' commitment to us, let us survey the word "compassion" as it appears in Matthew's gospel. Jesus says in Matthew 9:13:

> But go and learn what this means, "I desire compassion, and not sacrifice," for I did not come to call the righteous, but sinners.

Jesus was a friend of sinners and he called them to repentance. What he requires from us is a similar compassion of the heart rather than sacrifice or outward religious performance. Matthew 9:36 says of Jesus:

> When he saw the crowds, he had compassion on them, because they were harassed and helpless, like sheep without a shepherd. (NIV)

Jesus had compassion on people for he saw them as sheep without a shepherd. Has this kind of compassion ever stirred in you? When you are in a crowd, do you feel compassion for those around you or do you feel irritated? If a man standing next to you in a crowded train has bad breath, do you feel like recommending him mouthwash? Our thinking revolves around ourselves, so we don't know how to be compassionate. Compassion means to forget ourselves and to think of the needs of others. But we get annoyed when a man is leaning against us in the train or is holding on to the support bar and blocking our view.

Jesus was moved with compassion for people. Do we feel any compassion at all? By nature we are so self-centered that it's impossible for us to forget ourselves. But "compassion" and "mercy" come up in Matthew's gospel again and again, e.g. 5:7, 12:7, 14:14, 15:32, 18:27, 18:33 (twice), 20:34, 23:23. Compassion and mercy run through Matthew, bringing out the powerful motivation that works in the Lord Jesus. It is compassion that motivates his commitment to you and to me.

Returning to our question: Why did Jesus turn the other cheek? Was it because his Father had commanded him to? But obedience without compassion would be meaningless. Turning the other cheek must be motivated by compassion. If someone slaps us and we scream, "Go ahead! Slap me again!" our attitude would be wrong. Your turning the cheek would have meaning only if the other person sees compassion in your eyes.

Why do I need to show compassion when God is already all-compassionate? Isn't His compassion good enough? Again we are dealing with the motive. Do we know why we're doing what we're doing? What is it that motivates us to repent, forsake evil, and embrace good?

Moral choices and activities

In all this we are confronted with a choice between good and evil. It is a choice that takes us back to Genesis in the garden of Eden where Adam and Eve ate the forbidden fruit. One notable consequence of their disobedience is seen in Genesis 3:22:

> And the LORD God said, "The man has now become like one of us, knowing good and evil. He must not be allowed to reach out his hand and take also from the tree of life and eat, and live forever." (NIV)

Adam's decision to eat the forbidden fruit was consequential because he thereby gained the knowledge of good and evil. The word "know" doesn't mean intellectual knowledge but experiential understanding. Prior to disobeying God, Adam didn't know good and evil experientially; but in the act of disobeying God, he experienced good and evil. You only need to know the one to know the other. In doing what is evil, you get to know what is the good as its opposite. In doing what is the good, you get to know what is evil.

God doesn't need to do evil to know evil. He knows evil not because He has done evil but because evil has been done to Him, for all sin is ultimately done to God. Jesus knows evil too, not because he has done evil but because evil has been heaped on him and he was killed for our sins. No one knows evil as he, for no one has suffered the consequences of evil as he.

Every day we do three types of activity: physical, mental (intellectual), and spiritual. If an activity is purely physical or intellectual, it has no moral significance. By contrast, a spiritual activity has moral significance because it involves a choice between good and evil.

Let's imagine Adam and Eve in the garden. They see a peach tree and eat its fruit. This act has no moral significance because it is a physical activity in contrast to a spiritual activity. If I buy a drink at a store, is there any moral significance in whether I choose Coke, Pepsi, or root beer? This purely material decision has no moral significance because it has nothing to do with good and evil. A physical activity has no moral significance unless it is attached to, or is the consequence of a spiritual activity.

A physical choice—such as buying a brand of shampoo or choosing a color for my shirt—has no moral significance. Not even an intellectual activity such as guessing the weather or performing a math calculation has moral significance unless it is connected to a spiritual activity. The same with buying a book to learn French or Chinese. Whether I believe the universe is in an inflationary state after the Big Bang or in a deflationary state, has no moral significance.

Whether I believe in the theory of evolution also has no moral significance unless I use it to prove or disprove God's creation. In any case, this theory neither proves nor disproves creation because *evolution* is a process of life. It is logically invalid to prove the origin of life from a theory of the process of life. The evolutionary process proves nothing for or against creation because the origin of life has to be proved from something else. But when studied as theory, evolution has no intrinsic moral significance because it has nothing to do with good and evil.

Finally, intellectual belief in a Christian doctrine such as that Jesus died for you has no moral significance unless you draw from it something of spiritual value that pertains to your salvation. If we preach the gospel by telling people to believe in Jesus but without telling them to make a moral commitment, then we haven't preached the gospel at all. If your Christian profession is merely intellectual, you are not a Christian. If your faith makes no difference for good or evil in your life, you are in the same situation as Satan who also believes what you believe and more (James 2:19).

The way Peter preached the gospel is not the way it is preached today. His message in Acts 3 concludes with the words: "When God raised up his servant (Jesus), he sent him first to you to bless you by turning each of you from your wicked ways" (v.26). The blessing of eternal life requires us to make a moral decision to turn away from our "wicked ways". To be a Christian in the biblical sense is to forsake our evil ways and choose what is good. Then we can see good and evil in practical terms: compassion versus no compassion; love versus hate; a God-centered life versus a self-centered life; a lifestyle that cares for others versus one that grabs everything for oneself.

Turning the other cheek: exercising the nuclear option

To commit to God, we must know why we commit and to whom we commit. Why should I choose good over evil, or love over hate? I still need to understand the reasons for my choice.

If someone slaps me on the cheek, what options are available to me? One option is to slap him back, even two or three times. We may end up in a slugfest in which he slaps me, I slap him, he slaps me, I slap him, which is full-blown "eye for eye and tooth for tooth". I recently heard someone say that if everyone in society practices eye for eye, the world will be blind and eyeless!

The second option is non-retaliation: I refrain from hitting him back. In exercising self-control, my nerves are trembling, my muscles are tense, my fist is clenched, and I start counting "one, two, three" until my blood pressure subsides.

With the first option (retaliation), we are misusing the principle of "an eye for an eye" for personal retaliation, by returning evil for evil. Someone does evil to me, so I do evil to him, even paying back with interest. By adding my evil to his, I have multiplied evil. He may hit me a second or third time, so evil increases exponentially.

Is there a better way of dealing with the problem of evil? If I hit him back (retaliation), I have multiplied evil. If I don't hit him back (non-retaliation), I have kept evil at a constant level, neither increasing nor decreasing it.

But there is a third option: When someone slaps me, I turn the other cheek in love and compassion with the aim of overcoming his evil. Then he will be taken by surprise: "Why doesn't he hit me back? Why does he show me love and compassion after what I have done to him?" That is precisely what we want to achieve. In offering the other cheek, love begins to overpower him. Paul tells us that good is so powerful that it can overcome evil:

> Do not repay anyone evil for evil. Be careful to do what is right in the eyes of everybody. If it is possible, as far as it depends on you, live at peace with everyone. Do not take revenge, my friends, but leave room for God's wrath, for it is written: "It is mine to avenge; I will repay," says the Lord. On the contrary: "If your enemy is hun-

gry, feed him; if he is thirsty, give him something to drink. In doing this, *you will heap burning coals on his head.*" Do not be overcome by evil, but overcome evil with good. (Romans 12:17-21, NIV)

The expression "heap burning coals on his head" has been a subject of scholarly study. It means to cause a burning fire of shame, remorse, and regret. Because of your compassion, the other person has come to a burning sense of the wrong he has done you. So intense is his shame and remorse for having been your enemy that he feels the coals of fire burning on his head. The expression probably came from an old Egyptian proverb that describes the intensity of shame over having wronged someone who did not retaliate but responded to evil with love and good.

The one who loves with Christ's love is not weak but strong. The same cannot be said of the one who serves as a "carpet" for people to trample on. A person who is weak and passive has no power to overcome evil. The good we are talking about is active and powerful. It doesn't just endure abuse and insult, it goes one step further: If someone abuses you, you love him the more. Your enemy won't see this as weakness but as power! He might not react to you immediately but he will respect the power operating in you. You are not a punching bag but a powerful force that is overpowering evil.

What Paul is telling us to do—overcome evil with good—is something active, not passive. If you are passive, people will think you are weak and cowardly. But if you fight back with love, they won't know how to handle it. You have nuclear power that defeats conventional power. It is a divine power that confronts them. You are declaring an all-out war to defeat evil. This love is aggressive because it aims to conquer and not surrender.

This we cannot do except by God's power. When you let His power work in you, you will begin to experience amazing things. Accepting this challenge takes total commitment and choosing good over evil.

Remark: In turning the other cheek, we also need to be wise and to assess the situation on a case by case basis. It is no credit to the Christian when he behaves foolishly and without thinking. God's wisdom goes together with God's love so that we respond to situations appropriately and wisely.

Love overcomes: the case of my mother

Love and compassion come from God: "God's love has been poured into our hearts through the Holy Spirit who has been given to us" (Rom.5:5). This love is moral and spiritual. Love that has no moral element is not love. In the Bible, love is not a sentimental feeling but something that involves a decisive choice of good over evil. It is a commitment to love the unlovely. And because love is powerful enough to defeat evil, I don't have to retaliate, exchanging evil for evil. I overcome evil by God's goodness that has been poured into my life.

The more you apply this, the more you will see that God's love overpowers evil. The happy outcome is that I know why I am committed and why I turn the other cheek. It is a calculated act that, by God's goodness, overcomes evil in the other person.

When your enemy sees God's goodness in you, he will be convicted of his wronging. If he surrenders to good, we have won a battle against evil. If he refuses to repent, we will leave it to God to deal with him. Vengeance belongs to God the Judge. But whether the other person repents or not, I myself will not be defeated by evil, or give in to evil by retaliating. We are God's coworkers in the battle against evil, conquering evil by His love. It is achievable. All the way to judgment day, we will love those who hate and persecute us. Either they repent of their sins or God will deal with them on that day.

I know from experience that love conquers. Soon after I became a Christian, my parents rejected me. My mother made it clear to me that I wasn't welcome at home. When I came home during the school holidays, the very first question she asked was, "When are you leaving?" How's that for a welcome? But I was determined to love her to the end until God's love triumphs in her heart. Whenever my mother was unkind to me, I would go to the kitchen to do the dishes. She found this very strange because I previously would never do the dishes. What's more, in our family tradition, it wasn't a man's job to do the dishes. So this increased her bewilderment. And when she was unkind to me again, I would sweep the floors, do the grocery shopping, and bring home a present for her. When she continued to be unkind to me, I bought her some flowers. She didn't know how to handle this. No matter how badly she treated me, I loved her all the same.

Years later, she knelt beside me one day. With tears running down her face, she surrendered her life to God. Good had overcome evil. I will never forget what she said to me: "I gave you physical life, you gave me spiritual life." She channeled physical life to me, I channeled God's life to her by God's grace. We became very close after that. Before she came to God, I didn't have much affection for her, humanly speaking. In the beginning, it took commitment on my part to love her with God's love, for my heart had no human love or attachment for her. But later on, I loved her with God's love in a way I had never loved her before.

When she died a few years later, it took me a long time to recover. I knelt before God and said, "I don't understand. Why did you take her away? She was a new Christian who truly loved you. I was hoping she could do something for you before she passes away." To this day I do not have an answer to my question, but I do know that God's love was able to overcome the sin and evil in her heart. She admitted to being a sinful woman in her youth, yet she became a saint of God. Her whole life radiated the beauty of Christ, and I loved her ever so deeply.

I have witnessed the power of love that overcame the hardness in my mother's heart. Her heart was hard like rock, yet God was able to melt it. If love can win my mother, it can win anyone else because I know how hardened she was. I now understand the reasons for my commitment and my turning the other cheek, for I have experienced the power of God's love. I know it is real and that it works. I can love others because I know that God's love will triumph in every situation.

Chapter 8

The Goodness of God

For God or against God?

When you are confronted with a choice but don't make one, you have already made a choice. If it is a choice between good and evil, and you don't choose good, you have chosen evil. There is no middle ground between the two, neither in real life nor in the Bible. Jesus says, "Whoever is not with me is against me" (Lk.11:23).

Everywhere in the Old and New Testaments, choice confronts us. Right from the start, in the Garden of Eden, Adam and Eve had to choose between obedience and disobedience. Israel too was confronted with a choice again and again, even that between life and death:

> Today, I call heaven and earth to witness against you: I am offering you life or death, blessing or curse. Choose life, then, so that you and your descendants may live. (Dt.30:19, New Jerusalem Bible)

Moses, as God's spokesman, put before Israel the choice between life and death, blessing and a curse. We don't normally choose death, but if we don't choose life, we have chosen death. Not long afterwards, Israel was called again to make a choice, this time between Yahweh and the false gods of the nations, when Joshua said:

> But if serving Yahweh seems a bad thing to you, today you must make up your minds whom you do mean to serve, whether the gods whom your ancestors served beyond the River, or the gods of

the Amorites in whose country you are now living. As regards my family and me, we shall serve Yahweh. (Joshua 24:15, NJB)

Then all Israel declared their decision to serve Yahweh their God:

Far be it from us to desert Yahweh and to serve other gods! Yahweh our God was the one who brought us and our ancestors here from Egypt ... And Yahweh has driven all the nations out for us, including the Amorites who used to live in the country. We too shall serve Yahweh, for he is our God. (Joshua 24:16-18, NJB)

But Joshua did not believe them:

You will not be able to serve Yahweh, since he is a holy God, he is a jealous God who will not tolerate either your misdeeds or your sins. If you desert Yahweh and serve the foreigners' gods, he will turn and maltreat you anew and, in spite of having been good to you in the past, will destroy you. (Joshua 24:19-20, NJB)

The people pledged to serve Yahweh and not foreign gods, yet Joshua knew that they were still attached to the world, a world signified by the false gods of the region: the gods of fertility, harvest, and prosperity.

We don't need to read far into the Bible to see that their commitment was flimsy. By the time of 1 Kings, Israel had long turned away from Yahweh God. Chapter 18 records the confrontation on Mount Carmel between the prophet Elijah and 450 prophets of Baal. Elijah told the people of Israel to choose between Yahweh or Baal:

Elijah went before the people and said, "How long will you waver between two opinions? If Yahweh is God, follow him; but if Baal is God, follow him." But the people said nothing. (1 Kings 18:21)

In keeping silent, the people had already rejected God. Their earlier profession of commitment to God turned out to be no commitment, so Elijah said they were of two minds, wavering between two opinions. The rest of the story is well known, with Elijah calling down fire from heaven to consume the sacrifice on Mount Carmel.

Centuries earlier, in the time of Deuteronomy, the Israelites were told to choose life, but they eventually wavered between two opinions and ended up in death, even death of the nation. Centuries later, the northern kingdom was destroyed in 721 BC, and the southern kingdom in 587 BC. God's words are not empty utterances. When He tells us to choose life or death, good or evil, we have to take His word seriously.

Good requires more than right intention

One can be moral without being spiritual, but one cannot be spiritual without being moral. That is to say, one can be a so-called "good" person in society without being spiritual, but one cannot be spiritual in the true biblical sense without being a good person. It is parallel to what we said earlier, that you can be poor without being spiritual, but you cannot be spiritual without being poor. By "poor" we mean an attitude of not regarding our possessions as our own but as belonging to God.

Even if you are not committed to the good, it is still possible for you to mentally choose the good with your mind and declare it verbally with your mouth, as in the case of the Israelites when they stood before Joshua. They publicly declared their decision for God but Joshua knew it was just a mental choice, for in all the things they had been doing, they showed a strong attachment to Egypt, the symbol of the world. In the wilderness they were always hankering after the things they had left behind in Egypt. They had indeed left these things behind literally and physically, but their hearts had not abandoned them. Joshua knew that they hadn't broken free from the grip of the world, nor moved from evil to good, despite their public declaration of choosing the good.

Commitment takes more than right intention. Intention alone will not take you from evil to good. If you can do that by your own power, it would mean that you can save yourself by sheer determination. With sufficient will power, you can quit something like smoking, but no human effort can ever set you free from the power of evil. In your own strength it is impossible for you to be a Christian in the biblical sense, for it is a work that God does in you. Many are keenly aware that only God can rescue them from evil, yet they don't yield their lives to Him.

If indeed we are able to break free from evil in our own strength, we would be able to save ourselves and be the master of our lives. But because we cannot save ourselves, we are not our own masters.

A wrong concept of God as a killjoy

We are afraid that if God becomes the Lord of our lives, He will tell us to do what we don't want to do. We feel that the cost of passing from death to life, from evil to good, is too high because it involves surrendering the lordship of our own lives.

I once talked with a woman who was heartbroken after her boyfriend had ended their relationship. She felt she could still do something to win him back, but realistically she was deluding herself. Living in self-delusion is sad but at least it makes you feel that you still have some control of the situation.

She wasn't willing to trust in God for the future on this matter. When I asked why, she said, "What if God wants me to be single?" The thought of remaining single quite terrified her. It escapes me why she would think that God wants her to remain single. We often think that God wants the worst for us, and that if we put our lives into His hands, He will send us off to Alaska or the Sahara.

We have a strange concept of God, thinking that He delights in giving us the worst. Why do we think of God like this? I have spoken with many who are afraid to surrender their lives to God in case He might say, "The girl you like very much? Sorry, she's not for you."

To many Christians, God is a killjoy who takes away the things you like and gives you what you don't want. He takes away our money and reduces us to beggars (for the poor are blessed). Committing to God is risky, it is believed, because you will end up losing your girlfriend, your money, and everything you have, and then get something called eternal life that you can't see or touch. God forces you to give up the things you hold in your hands in exchange for something you don't see. But is God really like that?

I have counseled many who are afraid of what God might do if they should commit to Him. In their view, when you pray to God, He may tell you to get up and go to the Sahara. A common concept of God is that of a God who has nothing to do in heaven except to make life hard for you on earth, depriving you of nice things. If you think that God delights in depriving you of a wife or husband, or that He wants you to be clothed in rags, do you really know God?

Embodiments of good and evil

Like the Israelites, you may have made a commitment only with your mind, but you cannot serve God because your sense of values is distorted. If God takes you out of Egypt, you will complain in the wilderness, "Why did God take us out of Egypt, and what are we doing in the wilderness? In Egypt we had garlic, onions and leeks, but now we have this food called manna. God promised to give us a homeland but leaves it to us to conquer it with our blood, sweat and tears. How is this a free gift? We didn't come here to die." Then your spiritual perception becomes distorted, calling evil good and good evil (Isa.5:20).

Good and evil do not exist as isolated entities but are qualities that exist in people. There are good people and bad people, not isolated entities called good or bad. There is no such thing as a good place or a bad place in the moral sense. When we say a place is good, we mean it is nice and comfortable. A place is morally good or bad only if a good or bad person exercises his influence over it.

Good and evil exist in people but we are not the supreme embodiment of good and evil because we are not the highest order of spiritual beings. In the creation, we are the highest physical beings but not the highest spiritual beings. Hebrews 2:7, quoting Psalm 8:5, says that God made man a little lower than the angels. In the present age, angels are higher spiritual beings than us humans. And even among angels there are different ranks.

But we won't remain lower than angels forever, for it is God's plan to elevate those who choose good to be higher than the angels, even to the level of judging them (1Cor.6:3). That is because our adoption as children of God will by then be complete (Rom.8:23).

God, the supreme embodiment of good

The supreme embodiment of good or evil is found in spiritual beings higher than angels. The supreme embodiment of good is of course God himself. Jesus says to the rich young ruler, "Why do you ask me about what is good? There is only one who is good." (Mt.19:17) Here Jesus is implying that only God is good, but this is made explicit in a parallel passage, Luke 18:19: "Why do you call me good? No one is good except God alone." Jesus is saying that only one person in the universe, God Himself, can be properly called good. Indeed, God our Father is the source of all good things:

> Every good thing given and every perfect gift is from above, coming down from the Father of lights, with whom there is no variation or shifting shadow. (James 1:17, NASB)

God is the Father of lights. Genesis and the Psalms speak of the greater lights and the lesser lights, which are the heavenly bodies: the sun, the moon, the stars. God is the Father of lights because He is the Creator of all things, including earth, which is one planet among many. From another planet, earth looks like a star in the sky, a lesser light but still a light.

Just as God is the Creator of all things and the source of physical life and blessing, so He is the source of every good thing in the spiritual sphere. He is the Creator of physical life and the Giver of spiritual life, with the material sphere being a parallel of the spiritual sphere. There is no physical blessing that doesn't come from God: the beautiful flowers, the life-giving sunrays, and the foods we enjoy every day. Just as God gives us physical blessings, He gives us spiritual blessings.

There is no "variation or shifting shadow" in God who is the source of all good. God never changes. The heavenly lights such as the sun and the moon will eventually fade, but God's kindness, goodness, and faithfulness remain forever. People change but God never changes. People may be nice to you today and hate you tomorrow.

In committing to God our Father, we need to see His goodness and unchanging character before we can place our full confidence in Him. It is odd that humankind, so inconsistent and fluctuating, does not trust in God who is consistent and unwavering. The evil person reads his own character into his understanding of God's nature. Just as a criminal is suspicious of everyone, so the sinner reads his own character into God.

Good and evil, life and death

In Scripture, good and life are the two sides of a coin, and the same can be said of evil and death. Where there is good, there is life. Where there is evil, there is death. In talking about good and evil, we are talking about life and death. We are not discussing good and evil merely in moral terms but in terms of life and death. Just as God is the supreme embodiment of all good and therefore of all life, Satan is the supreme embodiment of all evil, so much so that the Bible simply calls him "the evil one" (1Jn.5:19).

Since God is the source of all good and is at the same time a spiritual being, *good* and *spiritual* cannot be separated. Correspondingly, because evil is embodied in Satan the evil one, we now see the spiritual dimension of evil. Evil is not just a matter of morality but of spirituality. That is why the Lord's prayer says "deliver us from evil" (Mt.6:13, NASB) or "deliver us from the evil one" (NIV).

Every decision for evil and every sin committed is, knowingly or unknowingly, a decision for the evil one and an advancement of his interests. Every sin we commit advances the kingdom of the evil one.

But not every act of good advances God's kingdom. The parallel is not exact. You can be moral without being spiritual but you cannot be spiritual without being moral. A moral act is not necessarily a spiritual act, but a spiritual act is always a moral act. An example of the former is seen in 1Cor.13:3: "If I give all my possessions to feed the poor and if I deliver my body to be burned, but do not have love, it profits me nothing." (NASB)

But if I show someone genuine love, that love will be expressed in some concrete manifestation called "good". If I give to the poor out of genuine love, it is because I have been made spiritual by God's grace.

But if I give to the poor for any other reason, even that of gaining moral satisfaction, it won't advance the kingdom of God.

Life and death as powers

Whereas good comes from God, evil is embodied in Satan, the evil one. Correspondingly, life comes from God because life cannot be separated from good. But death comes from Satan—though not only from him—for he has the "power of death" (Heb.2:14). If you choose God, you have chosen life. But if you don't choose God, you have chosen death.

To be saved is to pass from death to life. This requires the power of creation and the power of resurrection by which God creates life out of death. Being a Christian in the biblical sense is not just a matter of getting baptized or going to church, but of passing from death to life by God's life-giving power, the power of resurrection.

We tend to think of life and death as passive states of being but they are more properly understood as powers. It is easier for us to see life as a power because living beings are dynamic and are capable of thinking and communicating—I say something to you, you say something back.

But death is also a power insofar as you can inflict death on someone. Anything that destroys life is power. If you fire a gun, a bullet comes out with deadly power. In lethal injection, the poison injected into you represents the power of death at work in you.

Life and death are active powers, not passive states of being. When we say that God is the source of life, we don't mean that He is a container that holds life, but that He has the power to make us alive. When we say that Satan holds the power of death, we don't mean that he is a container that holds death, but that he can inflict death on others: "that by Jesus' death he might destroy him who holds the power of death—that is, the devil" (Heb.2:14). The devil holds the power of death insofar as he can inflict death on those who are under his power. We cannot go from evil to good in our own strength because we are dealing not with states of being but with powers that are too strong for us. It takes power to deal with power.

The Bible does not teach absolute dualism. By *dualism* we mean a balance of good and evil in the world. Some religions believe that two powers, good and evil, are in an epic but balanced war. *Absolute dualism* puts good and evil in equal balance whereas *relative dualism* assigns more power to good.

But not so in the Bible. Romans 12:21 tells us to "overcome evil with good," for good is *infinitely* more powerful than evil. This vital fact can be established not only from the Bible but also from the Christian's experience. Yet in the experience of many, evil is stronger than good. Paul describes a time in his life when he was unable to do the good he desired, but did the evil he hated (Rom.7:15). In his former state, evil was more powerful than good, and he was losing the battle to evil. In your own experience, is good stronger than evil, or are you losing the battle to evil? It is through commitment to God, who is the source of all good, that the good will always triumph in your life.

A correct concept of good and evil is vital for understanding the New Testament. It is the crucial concern of Romans. If you look up a concordance under *good* and *evil*, you will see the prominence of these words in the Bible and Romans in particular, a book that deals with faith, salvation and commitment.

Trusting God

Do you want to be set free from the power of evil and live under the power of good? Or are you afraid to live under God's power? Have you fallen for Satan's lie that God is not good but harsh? That is a strange lie to believe when the Bible says every good thing comes from God. If you believe that God is good, why do you hesitate to commit totally to Him? Maybe you don't really believe that God is good after all. The best way for you to know that every good thing comes from God is to experience this truth. The psalmist says, "O taste and see that the LORD is good" (Psalm 34:8).

I don't understand why people hesitate to commit to God, yet are willing to commit to someone in marriage. In a marriage you presumably give the other person everything you have and everything you are. If you are brave enough to entrust your life to a human being, where is your courage to trust in God who never changes and is the fountain of all good? Has anyone ever given his or her only son for your sake? Has your spouse ever done anything for you on that level? He or she might say "I love you" and other endearing words, but human beings can change. Satan's lie must have worked because you don't really believe that God is good—at least not as good as your spouse or your friend.

You trust your doctor enough to pay him or her a fortune to stick a surgical knife into you. Perhaps God's only mistake was not to send us a hefty bill! Paul told the Corinthians that he did not exercise his right to receive money from them, but instead gave of himself to them without charge. Is it because God's goodness is so generous that we take it for granted? Does God need to send us a hefty bill before we see that He is good? It is human psychology to think that something is good only if we have to pay good money for it. Why do we find it hard to commit to God when He has been so generous to us? Do we take Him and His gifts for granted? We entrust our lives to human doctors even though they make mistakes, sometimes fatal ones. God never makes a mistake, so why don't we trust Him totally?

Chapter 9

Overcoming Evil with Good

You have taken away the key of knowledge

In Luke 11:52 we see Jesus' strong denunciation of lawyers:

> Woe to you lawyers! For you have taken away the key of knowledge.
> You did not enter yourselves, and you hindered those who were
> entering. (ESV)

Who were the lawyers whom Jesus denounced in such strong terms?
They were the specialists in the Old Testament law, a law which gov-
erned every facet of Jewish life, including what one may eat. It had
detailed regulations on marriage, business transactions, the buying and
selling of land, and even dealings between Jews and Gentiles. These
lawyers were similar to modern lawyers except that they were experts
in the Torah of the Hebrew Bible rather than British or American law.

Why did the Lord Jesus denounce them so strongly? It is because
they had "taken away the key of knowledge." They weren't using the
key to get in, yet were hindering those who wanted to get in.

The question of entering in, or not entering in, has a lot to do with
the topic of commitment. You may be an expert in the Bible (as were
the lawyers) but that doesn't mean you have made a commitment to
God. Many theologians find themselves in a similar situation today:
Despite their head knowledge, they have not entered into, or allowed
others to enter into, a knowledge of God.

The meaning of "know"

In the Bible, the word "know" or "knowledge" doesn't mean intellectual knowledge. Knowledge in the Bible is not mental knowledge but experiential knowledge. Knowing God is not just knowing *about* God but having a living relationship with Him. We are so accustomed to taking "know" in the intellectual or cognitive sense that we often fail to see its biblical meaning.

You may know about Angela Merkel in terms of her biographical details—that she was born in West Germany, that she grew up in East Germany, that she became Chancellor of Germany—but that doesn't mean that you know her directly and personally.

Jesus was telling the lawyer-theologians that they had the key to knowing God, yet didn't use it to enter into a relationship with God. More than that, they hindered others from entering into a knowledge of God. Maybe they hindered them by setting a poor moral example for them. Maybe they didn't know God personally and weren't able to introduce others to God. Or maybe they didn't want others to know God, for it would be embarrassing for them if the ordinary people had a living relationship with God and they didn't.

Whether you enter or don't enter into a living relationship with God is ultimately an issue of commitment. Commitment is not merely an intellectual assent by which you say, "I believe this and accept that." We don't normally speak of intellectual knowledge as an "entering in," but we do view commitment as an "entering in," for example, entering into the commitment of marriage. "Entering in" has to do with action, motion, and commitment.

What is the key of knowledge?

If you have the key of knowledge yet don't enter in, you are in the same situation as the lawyers. Having the key of knowledge places a heavy responsibility on you before God.

A key is vital because without it, you cannot open a door unless it is already open or someone opens it for you. If you insert the key and turn it, you will get in. If you don't insert the key, or if you don't have the key, you won't get in.

So why didn't the lawyers use the key if they had it? Because it involved a high cost. When you are entering in, there are certain things you cannot take along with you. It is harder for a rich man to enter the kingdom of God than for a camel to go through the eye of a needle. It takes total transformation to enter the kingdom because we normally do not abandon the things we like. Yet there were certain things the lawyers didn't want to leave behind. Likewise, most of us want to bring along our old sins and habits when we enter into commitment. If we are told to abandon the things we don't want to give up, we wouldn't be so keen to go in. You may have the key yet you don't want to leave some things behind. It is tragic when someone knows how to enter into a living relationship with God, yet refuses to make use of that knowledge.

When you take an international flight and go through airport inspection, sometimes you worry if you can bring in certain goods that you have paid good money for. One time I was returning to Canada with some presents. I had a pack of the highest quality dried meat that I had bought while passing through Taiwan. At that time, I didn't know enough about customs regulations; and on that particular trip, I had to pass through Hawaii en route to Canada. And do you know what happened? My heart sank when the customs officer took my beautiful bag of dried meat, the lovely present I was going to give to someone, and threw it into the garbage bin right in front of me! I thought to myself, "Hey, I'm not visiting the United States. Just give it back to me, and I'll go by another way!" Of course I couldn't do that. I learned the hard way that you cannot bring certain foods into or through the United States. The same would have happened in Canada, though I didn't know it at the time.

Similarly, when entering the kingdom of God, we need to look at the things that are precious to us. We have spent considerable time and effort acquiring them, and feel that they are inherently good. There are other things we don't mind leaving behind because they are obviously bad and shouldn't be brought in. That part doesn't bother us, and we don't make a fuss over them. In deciding whether to take the step of commitment, the things that are most problematic are the things that we feel are not inherently bad, so we don't understand why we're not allowed to take them along.

I am still wondering what was wrong with the bag of delicious meat. And before you toss it into the bin, at least let me have some of it right on the spot. In the matter of commitment, many people are like that. "Before I make my commitment, I will enjoy the world a bit more before it's too late." We have many personal reasons for not entering into commitment.

Self-centeredness versus loving God

What then is the key of knowledge? The clues are found in the words *key* and *knowledge*. Jesus doesn't explicitly say what the key of knowledge is, but from the word *knowledge* it is connected to something the lawyers knew very well: the teaching of the Bible. In fact these lawyers had a specialist knowledge of the Bible. Since this knowledge is a key, and since the Bible is the word of God, the key of knowledge opens the door for entering into a relationship with God.

The key of knowledge is loving God with one's whole being. That is in fact the sum and essence of the whole Law, as Deuteronomy and the gospels tell us. The lawyers knew this well. They knew that the law isn't really about fulfilling this or that regulation, but about loving God with one's whole being. But did they love God totally? As we see in Jesus' denunciation of the lawyers and Pharisees in Matthew 23, they were lovers of self, not lovers of God.

It is absolutely vital for us to leave behind the love of the self—the dominant controlling factor in our lives since the day we were born—and to enter into a life characterized by love for God. How else can we taste and see that the Lord is good?

We have to pass from evil to good. What then is evil and what is good? We now see that evil, in biblical teaching, is the self-centeredness which is so much a part of our nature. We often justify our self-centeredness by saying that it is necessary in life and that we need to be realistic, having our feet planted firmly on the ground and not our heads lost in the clouds. But no matter how we justify it, self-centeredness is ultimately looking out for number one: *me.*

This way of thinking has been controlling us all our lives. We instinctively put ourselves and our interests above those of everyone else. Our minds have been trained to think: "My interests are more important than yours. In a choice between you and me, I always choose me. It is not in my nature to be self-giving because that would put my interests below those of God and His people."

As I said, we cannot pass from evil to good by ourselves because that is not in our nature. Christianity is not a "religion" in the usual sense of the word. Every religion tells you to do good, but the problem is that we often don't know what is the good. The gulf between good and evil is so vast that you cannot pass from evil to good except through a radical transformation. Your whole life has to change totally from being self-centered to being God-centered.

In the Bible, evil is not necessarily an act of murder or adultery. *The root of evil is the love of self.* The love of self expresses itself, for example, in the love of money. If you don't love the self, you wouldn't love money. But you love money because money can do many things for the self. The love of self is the root of all evil, for it gives rise to all other sins. Why does a person rob? He doesn't care if the victim loses his life savings so long as "I" get the money. Why does a person slander? What does he gain from it? Nothing, unless by destroying someone's reputation, he gains something for himself.

A good act is not necessarily good

When the Bible talks about good and evil, and when Pharisees talk about good and evil, and when the world religions talk about good and evil, the meaning is not the same. We must not be misled by the similarity of words.

If I give money to the poor, is it a good act? Yes, according to most religions. But according to the Bible, *not necessarily so.* But isn't helping the poor always good? It is not necessarily good because it may have been motivated by pride, selfishness, or ulterior motives. The act may appear good but not so in God's eyes if it is motivated by self-love. Having a good feeling from a moral deed doesn't make it a good deed. The Bible has a deeper definition of good than we can find anywhere else.

The scribes and Pharisees knew the Law. As we saw in Deuteronomy 30, the Law forces us to choose between good and evil, life and death, blessings and a curse. The scribes and Pharisees knew that the key to life is choosing good and loving God with our whole being. But what did these lawyer-theologians do? They abandoned this vital truth and took away the key, by redefining good and evil in terms of keeping or not keeping the Law! In this new definition, keeping the Law is good, not keeping the Law is evil. This is something that Jesus severely condemns.

With this definition, when someone does a good act, he is good, for goodness has been defined as acts of good. This has led many to believe that you only need to keep the Law to be saved. If the Law tells you not to work on the Sabbath, you don't work on the Sabbath. If the Law tells you not to eat pork, you don't eat pork. If you don't eat pork or work on the Sabbath, you are good. But it doesn't take a deep thinker to see that refraining from eating pork doesn't prove that one is good. Good is not the sum total of good deeds.

In the Bible, good is defined not by what you do but *what you are*. That is the essence of the key of knowledge! What you are depends on whether you love God with all your heart and whether He is the center of your life. If you are good, everything you do will be good. A good tree produces good fruit but a bad tree produces bad fruit (Mt.7:17-18; Lk.6:43-44). When you break open a seemingly good fruit from a bad tree, you may find worms inside. Doing good deeds doesn't prove that you are good. In God's sight, our good deeds are not good unless they stem from a good nature.

Here we see conflicting definitions of good. The scribes and lawyers equate good with good deeds, and define good deeds in terms of doing the Law. The Lord Jesus rejects this teaching because it means that one can do good deeds without being committed to good or to God who is the source and essence of good.

When I was a non-Christian, I did many good deeds and everyone thought I was a nice guy. If a poor guy got bullied, I would beat up the bully. It made me feel good to rescue the weak and downtrodden, but my good deeds only catered to my pride and ego. At that time, I didn't know that good is not the sum total of good deeds.

The words may be the same but the substance is different. When you talk to people about being a Christian, they would often say, "But every religion tells you to do good." Even Satan will tell you to do good for he disguises himself as an angel of light (2Cor.11:14). Would an angel of light, even if he is an imposter, tell you to do evil? Satan will tell you to do good because it will make you feel good, or feel that you are moral by your own power, and this could lead to your downfall.

Grasp the vital difference: Good, when taught in the wrong way, can destroy you by catering to your pride. Some of the most difficult people to reach with the gospel are the moral people who feel that they are good and don't need the gospel. *Religion is the worst enemy of spirituality.*

Whereas religion is mere morality, spirituality has to do with our relationship with God. What we are promoting is not mere morality but a relationship with a God who is good and transforms us from evil to good. All this is achieved by God's work, which is why salvation is by grace. Baptism is not about joining a religion or even the Christian religion, but proclaiming that we have died to the self-centered life so that God alone is now the center of our lives.

The power to "overcome" evil

We have looked at the motivation of commitment, and this takes us back to Romans 12:21: "Do not be overcome by evil but overcome evil with good." Because theology can be abstract, I am using the language of good and evil to make things easy to grasp. If you understand the biblical meaning of good and evil—a theme that spans the Bible from Genesis to Revelation—you will have come a long way towards understanding the deep things of the Bible. In Romans 12:21 we see Paul's skill in presenting profound truths in simple language.

Let us look at the word "overcome" in Romans 12:21 ("overcome evil with good"). If we grasp this word, we will understand the deep things of theology. I touched on this topic when I pointed out that the Bible speaks of a dualism between good and evil—between God and Satan—but it is not an absolute dualism. That is because God is always in control.

In living the Christian life, it is crucial for us to know that God is always in control. Because His power is overwhelmingly superior to Satan's, good will always be able to overcome evil. I stress "be able to" because good doesn't necessarily overcome evil even though it is able to. That is because you and I might not be working on the side of good. If you cooperate with evil, evil will triumph over good in your life.

But Satan will never triumph over God because God's plan can never be defeated. The Bible speaks of God's predetermined plan of salvation, which is the essence of predestination. Biblical predestination is different from Calvinistic predestination but I won't discuss this now. Biblical predestination is possible because good is always more powerful than evil, for God is more powerful than the evil one. Satan can never frustrate God's predestined plan. Predestination is God's plan for the world, for mankind, for you and me, and no power of evil can ever defeat it.

"Nike" and life

God's overwhelming power is seen in the tiny word "overcome". It is not a tiny word in English but it is tiny in Greek: *nikē* has only four letters. I would like you to focus on *nikē*, not because I own any shares in the Nike sports company (I don't own any), but because this Greek word means triumph, victory, and overcoming.

We can understand *nikē* from two angles: God overcoming the evil one by His goodness, and our overcoming evil with good by God's power. These are the two sides of the coin though the latter involves our cooperation and co-working with God.

Salvation is achieved when God overcomes evil with His goodness. We were formerly under the power of the evil one, but God has set us free by His power and opened for us a way to enter into His life and goodness. This is salvation in a nutshell. The New Testament speaks of God's goodness on several levels. Paul says:

> For just as through the disobedience of the one man the many were made sinners, so also through the obedience of the one man the many will be made righteous. (Romans 5:19, NIV)

This passage may seem difficult but it boils down to this: goodness is obedience whereas evil is disobedience. Goodness stems not from a good act but from a good person. Ultimately the contrast is not between an act of obedience and an act of disobedience but between a good person and a bad person. Jesus is the good person whose act of obedience overcomes an act of disobedience by a bad person, namely Adam who was self-centered and wanted to be equal with God. Adam did not commit sins such as stealing or murder but he sinned by disobeying God out of his self-centeredness.

The goodness in Christ overcomes the evil in Adam. Good is so much more powerful than evil that there is no balance between the two powers. Romans 5 says that God's goodness is "much more" than a match for evil. In the whole chapter, the powerful phrase "much more" occurs several times, for example: "Since we have now been justified by his blood, how much more shall we be saved from God's wrath through him!" (Rom.5:9)

Three metaphors of overcoming

The Bible has several metaphors for good overcoming evil. The good of God overcomes the evil of Satan on several levels. In all these metaphors, *nikē* brings out the aspect of overpowering. If you defeat your adversary in a court of law, or in athletic competition, or in military combat, the Bible would describe that as *nikē* (overcoming), which is the word used in Romans 12:21.

The most powerful example of *nikē* is the resurrection, by which life overcomes death. Death and evil are the two sides of a coin, as are life and good. When we say that good overcomes evil, we are saying that life overcomes death. That is resurrection! Baptism signifies life over-coming death, and the new life in Christ overcoming the old self. Paul combines these metaphors in his letter to the Colossians:

> And you, who were dead in your trespasses and the uncircumcision of your flesh, God made alive together with him, having forgiven us all our trespasses. (Colossians 2:13, ESV)

This is a metaphor yet more than a metaphor, for Paul is talking about life overcoming death. You were dead in your transgressions when you were controlled by the flesh, which is self-centered by nature. But this death has been overcome in Christ by the power of the resurrection at baptism.

The first metaphor, then, is that of life overcoming death. The second metaphor is seen in the next verse: "… by canceling the record of debt that stood against us with its legal demands. This he set aside, nailing it to the cross." (Col.2:14, ESV)

This is a legal metaphor. When you are living in sin, there is a legal claim on you, just as a creditor who lends you money has a legal claim on you because of your debt. The Bible depicts sin as debt; compare "forgive us our debts" (Mt.6:12) and "forgive us our sins" (Lk.11:4).

At the cross Jesus overcame evil, broke the bondage that kept us in debt, and set the captives free. Your debt which kept you in the grip and power of the evil one, has been overcome by the cross of Jesus Christ, who canceled the debt by his goodness and mercy.

In the Old Testament, "atonement" comes from a Hebrew word which means to cover. The sin of disobedience is *covered* by an act of righteousness, not in the sense of its being hidden but in the sense of its being cancelled. When we say that a debt is *covered* by a payment, we mean exactly that. We don't mean that the debt is hidden from sight.

The third metaphor is seen in yet the next verse, Colossians 2:15: "He disarmed the rulers and authorities and put them to open shame, by triumphing over them in him." This is a war metaphor because "disarmed" has to do with weapons. This is *nikē* in war. Whereas the previous metaphor has to do with overcoming an adversary in a court of law (the cross of Christ cancels our debt and gives us legal victory), now God has won the war against evil by defeating the hostile powers that kept us in bondage.

Matthew 12, Mark 3, and Luke 11 all have an interesting story of a strong man, Satan, who is overpowered by someone even stronger. In Lk.11:22, "overpowered" (*nikaō*) is the verb form of *nikē*. God's work in Christ defeats a most formidable enemy, Satan, and gives us victory over the power of evil.

God's unfathomable goodness

It is one thing to understand these things intellectually but another to experience them. Have you experienced the transition from death to life? Have your legal bonds been broken by God's power? Have you been set free from Satan by entering into a commitment that has God as the center of your life? In all this, we see God's commitment to us in His setting us free. His wonderful goodness to us never fails to boggle my mind:

> He who did not spare his own Son but gave him up for us all, how will he not also with him graciously give us all things? (Rom.8:32)

Why is it so hard for us to commit to God when He is so good to us? If God did not spare His only Son but gave him up for you and me, will He not together with Christ "graciously" give us all things? Will God hold back anything that is good for you?

> If you then, who are evil, know how to give good gifts to your children, how much more will your Father who is in heaven give good things to those who ask him! (Mt.7:11, ESV)

Parents think they are giving good things to their children when in fact these things may be ruining them. But God doesn't make that kind of mistake because He knows what is good for us. We don't always know what is good for others, and we sometimes mess up people's lives with our good intentions. But will God withhold from us anything that is truly good for us? If you have trouble committing to a God who is willing to give His Son for your sake, you will have trouble committing to anyone in the world.

Paul speaks with triumphant confidence in God's love in Christ: "Who shall separate us from the love of Christ?" (Rom.8:35) No one can separate us from Christ's love and his commitment to us except we ourselves. Yet so many Christians are living in spiritual poverty. God withholds spiritual riches from those who refuse to commit, or they will never arrive at commitment. That would be the greatest disaster of all, for it would mean that God confirms them in their destruction.

More than conquerors

God has overcome evil and He calls us to overcome evil with His good (Rom.12:21). All good comes from God, hence it is only by His good that we overcome evil. Romans 12:21 sums up the essence of the Christian life. Paul is a master teacher, yet most of his readers don't understand what he teaches. The Christian life is about *victory*. It is a marvelous life, but you wouldn't have guessed it by looking at most Christians today, who are crawling on hands and knees.

I once saw on television a runner trying to finish an Olympic marathon. I don't know if you have seen that terrible incident. When you compete in a marathon, you must pace yourself according to your stamina so that you can make it to the end. But this runner pressed himself too hard in the beginning, so he staggered in the last lap and collapsed less than 100 yards from the finish line. He got back on his feet and staggered for another 10 or 15 feet before collapsing again. The spectators were shouting, "You're almost there!" He got back up on his feet and staggered back and forth like a drunkard, falling again and again. No one could assist him because that would disqualify him. The spectators could only watch this poor man from their seats. Millions more around the world were watching this wrenching struggle. In the end, he didn't make it, falling short of the finish line by a few yards. He got up one last time and collapsed. He just couldn't make it.

I wonder how many Christians are struggling like that. Your heart goes out to them for this is not the Christian life. Romans 8:37 says "we are more than conquerors" or "we overwhelmingly conquer". It is good to conquer, but Paul says we are to *overwhelmingly* conquer.

Some time ago, a church in Hong Kong was offering something called "S.T." I asked what it stood for and was told that it stood for Survival Training. I asked why it was called Survival Training and they said, "Because it is important to survive spiritually." I agree it is important to survive spiritually, but if I read my Bible correctly, the Christian life is not about survival but about overwhelming victory! Is it because we lack the confidence to win that we talk of survival?

If you aim for a C in an exam, you might get a D. It may be better to aim for an A and get a B. My point is that if you aim only for survival, you might not even survive. I don't want to criticize the term Survival Training. I do recognize it is important to survive, but we have to go beyond that, for when we commit to our all-conquering God, we aim for victory, not just survival.

The word *nikē* (victory, overcoming) occurs frequently in Revelation, the last book of the Bible, in a way that stands in stark contrast to the runner who started the marathon beautifully but collapsed in the final and most critical lap in which most runners go flat out. To use the language of driving, the people in the book of Revelation open up the throttle, pressing their feet to the floorboard.

Isn't the Christian life supposed to be like that? I am afraid that the last lap is where many Christians will fail. But how does the Bible conclude? With a flat-out run in the last lap! In the New Testament, the word *nikē* occurs most often in Revelation. In this final book of the Bible, the verb form of *nikē* (*nikaō*, to overcome, Rom.12:21) occurs 16 times in the Greek text of Revelation, which is more than in the rest of the New Testament combined. That is how the Christian life ought to be lived, from strength to strength, and victory to victory!

God has given us the power not just to survive but to run the last lap. Live the Christian life such that even if you're going full speed now, when you reach the last lap, you leave the best for last! Paul's life is triumphant all the way. Did he ever say, "I am close to the finish line, so please drag me through the final few yards."? His last words in the Bible are:

> I have fought the good fight, I have finished the race, I have kept the faith. Henceforth there is laid up for me the crown of righteousness, which the Lord, the righteous judge, will award to me on that Day. (2Tim.4:7-8, ESV)

You can see the joy beaming in Paul's face. Can you finish the race like that? Only with faith and total commitment can you live a victorious and dynamic life that overcomes.

Chapter 10

Experiencing the Reality of God

God's commitment to us is *grace* whereas our commitment to God is *faith*. But today the word "faith" has been so diluted as to mean creedal or intellectual assent, more or less, that we need to find another word that accurately conveys the biblical meaning of faith. Indeed, many New Testament authorities now explain faith as "commitment".[6]

In the church over the centuries, *faith* has come to mean accepting certain doctrinal statements to be true. As a result, "I believe in Jesus" has come to mean, "I believe that there was a person called Jesus, that he died for me, that he rose again." This is *faith* in the church today. While these creedal statements are important, merely accepting them to be true is not the full meaning of faith in the New Testament. Certainly it is crucial to believe that Jesus died for us and rose again,

---

[6] *Zondervan Bible Dictionary*, article "Faith": "Faith is not to be confused with a mere intellectual assent to the doctrinal teachings of Christianity, though that is obviously necessary. It includes a radical and total commitment to Christ as the Lord of one's life". *Dictionary of the Bible* (John McKenzie, S.J.), article "Faith" (p.268): "The scope of the faith demanded by Isaiah shows that faith was a total commitment to Yahweh, a renunciation of secular and material resources, a seeking of security in the saving will of God alone." *Nelson's Illustrated Bible Dictionary* begins the article "Faith" as follows: "Faith—a belief in or confident attitude toward God, involving commitment to His will for one's life." See also *The New Interpreter's Dictionary of the Bible*, article "Faith, Faithfulness," sub-article "Faith as assent and commitment" (vol.2, pp.416-417).

but this alone is not saving faith. The devil knows correct doctrine too (James 2:19) but that does not save him.

The word *commitment* conveys the fact that in the Bible, saving faith is not just believing something to be true, but is a response to God that involves the whole person, not just his intellect or emotions but everything in him. It is a response that holds nothing back from God. God has given us everything, so we give Him our everything. Saving faith is a response to God which is expressed in total commitment and seen in works. James is not afraid to speak of *works* (a widely abused and misunderstood term) when he says, "Faith without works is dead" (James 2:17,20,26). A dead faith saves no one.

The Reality of God

We come back to the crucial question of why we should commit to God in the first place. How do we know that God is real to the extent that we have the confidence to commit to Him without reserve? Whether we commit to God depends on whether we are convinced that He is worth committing to. That in turn depends on whether we are convinced that He is real. We wouldn't commit to a fictitious person or ideology though some people are willing to do just that.

The question of God's reality is so vast that it would be overly ambitious of us to try to cover it in one chapter. But we will attempt just that, by looking at the evidence for God's existence briefly but I hope not too superficially. I will give you some lines of evidence for God's reality for you to think about, without laboring on the individual points.

1. God is revealed through the creation

What is the basis of our belief that God is real? What are the lines of evidence for establishing our case? The evidence before us is vast if we would open our minds and examine the facts. The Bible, right from Genesis 1:1, starts with the creation. Paul says that God has revealed Himself in His creation, and that we only need to look at it:

For since the creation of the world His invisible attributes, His eternal power and divine nature, have been clearly seen, being understood through what has been made, so that they are without excuse. (Romans 1:20, NASB)

When I first arrived in Montreal, I was deeply impressed by the pastor of a Russian church in Montreal. I asked him if he had become a Christian in the West but he said he started to know God in Soviet Russia. I said, "So you were brought up in the teaching that God does not exist?" He said, "Yes, but no matter what they told us about God's existence, the more I looked at creation, the more I was convinced that there has to be a God."

I asked him how that came about and he said, "I would be sitting in my astrophysics class listening to lectures on the universe and the stars. I pondered on the vastness and the orderliness of the universe, the way things move with precision and perfect timing, the enormous energies of the things in the universe, and the vast distances. In astronomy we talked about infinity, which is eternity, and eternity is about God." That left a deep impression on him.

When you look up at space, you are looking at infinity and eternity. Its limitlessness boggles the mind. Every time this Russian pondered about it, he would say to himself, "There has to be a God!" He also knew it was for political reasons that his teachers were saying there is no God. It was politics, not science.

So I asked him, "What's the rest of your story? You didn't become a Christian just by sitting in your astronomy class, did you?" He said no, he didn't. Although he knew that there has to be a God, he didn't know enough about Christianity.

He was also patriotic. When Germany invaded Russia in the Second World War, he was a young fighter pilot in the Soviet air force. The first thing the Germans did was to send wave after wave of bombers to destroy the planes on the airfields. They indeed destroyed most of the Soviet air force on the ground. As a result, the Germans had air control in the first phase of the war against the Soviet Union.

This Russian was grounded because he had no plane to fly, but that was also true of most other Soviet pilots. He would sit next to the air-field, reading the newspapers.

The Germans were advancing in their *blitzkrieg* or lightning war-fare, pushing rapidly across Russia. Before long they were besieging Leningrad on one front and advancing on Stalingrad on another.

While reading the papers, this young Russian became more and more agitated. So he said to his commanding officer, "Why am I sitting here? The Germans are invading our country and we are sitting here with no planes to fly. We have to get into the war effort."

The officer looked at the young man all heated up and ready to do combat, and said, "Are you willing to fight in infantry?" He said "yes" and was soon sent to the front.

Soon he found himself really at the front, eyeball to eyeball with German soldiers. For the first time he knew what fear was. The advan-tage of flying a plane is that you don't see your enemy's face or stare into his eyes. You fire at him from a distance. So it was a shock to him when he stood up in his trench and saw a German soldier in another trench. He thought to himself, "I have no quarrels with him, yet he's supposed to shoot me and I'm supposed to shoot him! Is this what life is all about?"

One day as he was standing in a trench, he pulled his cap over his eyes and began to pray. This was the first step he took to knowing God. He slowly pushed up his cap, hoping that no one had seen him pray-ing. A fellow soldier looked at him and smiled, so he was embarrassed and looked the other way. But the other said to him, "You were pray-ing, weren't you?"

"Me praying?"

"Yes, you were praying! Admit it!"

"Yes, I was praying."

"So was I! That makes the two of us!"

How interesting! All their lives they had been taught there is no God. But this Russian said to me, "You would be surprised at how many soldiers in the Soviet army prayed!"

And what happened next? He was captured when the German forces breached the Soviet lines. As was often the case, the Soviet soldiers didn't have enough ammunition to defend themselves. They were surrounded, isolated, and taken prisoner. He himself was taken to a prisoner-of-war camp in Germany. Towards the end of the war, he was transferred to a camp located in Nazi-occupied Austria. This part of Austria was subsequently taken by the Allied forces. This whole group of Soviet prisoners, hundreds of thousands of them, were then transferred from German hands into the custody of the western Allies. The Americans opened the camps for relief supplies and even organized gospel outreach activities. Some preachers came into the camp to reach out to the Soviet prisoners. This Russian received some tracts, and committed his life to God.

There were three stages in all this. First he saw God's glory in creation. Second, he began to pray. Third, he heard the gospel which he had never heard before, though he had known something about Christ.

This Russian came to realize that the only way for you to reach out to the Creator of the universe is for Him to reach out to you. We may want to know God but God is far more determined to know us! As soon as this Russian heard the gospel, he recognized the truth. He not only believed and committed his life to God, he became the pastor of a Russian church.

Jesus Christ and the creation

Yahweh God is the only creator (Isa.44:24) whereas Jesus Christ is the "firstborn of all creation" (Col.1:15). It was "in" Christ and "through him and for him" that all things were created by God (v.16). When we meditate on the universe and its eternal design, we are drawn to its Creator—the one and only God—through His Son Jesus Christ, who is the only way to God our Father (John 14:6).

In Scotland I was debating with a young man from India who believed in many gods. Indeed I was told that in India, there are more gods than people. With over a billion people in India, there must be many Hindu gods! This young man told me that there are many roads to God, a familiar idea in Indian philosophy. I said to him, "Please tell me which road leads you directly to God. What is the point of saying there are theoretically many roads to God unless you can point me to one specific road that will take me directly to God? I already know that Jesus is the way to God. If you don't come to God through Jesus, you won't come to Him at all. I challenge you to find another way to God, and when you have found it, come and tell me that you have met with God."

He replied, "There are many holy men in India." I said, "I won't argue with that but whether these holy men have come to God or not is another matter. I have already told you I have come to God through Jesus Christ, and I assure you that you too will come to know God if you take this road. If you believe there are theoretically a hundred ways to God, go and find one specific way." He thought about it and eventually became a Christian himself. That was partly a result of the powerful witness in the lives of other Christians, something which we will look at later.

The first point is that God is revealed in His creation. Look at a living flower and its beautiful design. If a craftsman had made you an artificial flower of gold, pearls and diamonds, it would not compare with the splendor of a living flower. When you place the two side by side, there is no competition in color, shape, vibrancy and fragrance. The other day I picked a flower on the island of Cheung Chau in Hong Kong, and I stood there admiring it. It was incredibly beautiful with a white trumpet shape, golden streaks, subtle shades of yellow, and even fragrance!

When you look at an artificial flower made of gold and diamonds, doesn't it tell you something about the craftsman's talent, intelligence and creativeness? Some people admire works of craftsmanship and are willing to pay thousands of dollars for one. The commercial value of its constituent parts in terms of gold and diamonds may not be very high, so what you are paying for is its artistic beauty.

Is it because we can pick a flower for free that we don't give it a second glance? If an artificial flower tells you something about its designer, how much more a living flower about its Creator?

If a flower can be so impressive, what about a bird or a fish? There was a time when I didn't know much about the splendor of the underwater world. But when you go scuba diving, what you see below the surface will really open your eyes. You put on your mask and oxygen tanks, and dive down 20 feet, 30 feet, maybe 100 feet. I once took my wife snorkeling in the Caribbean, and although snorkeling doesn't give you the same view as scuba diving, she was already dazzled by what she saw in the coral reefs.

When you go scuba diving, you can get close to the corals and see the fish swarming around you and staring into your goggles. They are as curious about me as I am about them. The colors, the shapes and the diversity of the fish are amazing. If you take a sheet of paper and draw on it a sea creature out of your imagination, adding a bit of yellow here and a bit of green there, with a hint of blue, there is a good chance you will draw something similar to what already exists underwater. Flip through a book on marine biology and you will see all kinds of interesting creatures. One of them might be what you have drawn on that sheet of paper.

With some fish, you cannot easily tell which end is head and which is tail. Sometimes it is hard to distinguish the eyes or know how many eyes there are. There are fish that catch other fish with something that looks like a fishing rod which extends from its head with what looks like a bait dangling at the end. Fish that fish for fish?

There are fish that shoot jets of water from below the surface to knock down overflying insects. Anyone who has studied trigonometry, projectile motion and fluid mechanics would know just how complex it is. Who taught the fish trigonometry and how did it acquire its skill? According to the theory of evolution, the species of fish evolved in that direction due to survival and selection. But wouldn't the species starve to death long before it evolves to the point of being able to shoot down insects?

If anyone could go through life looking at creation, yet not see the glory of the Creator, he or she must be suffering from a spiritual ailment. How can anyone look at all this and not see anything?

Many of us have been brought up in the theory of evolution. In China I had the privilege of being "liberated" for seven years. Part of that liberated life was to be ingrained with evolution and dialectical materialism. In one of my classes, a red guard asked the teacher how life originated: "You're teaching us evolution, so I would like to go back to the time prior to evolution and ask where did life come from?" His point was that if life comes from life according to the natural law as posited by Pascal, where did the first life form come from? That question was more than the teacher could handle, so he said, "That's easy. Life comes from non-life."

The student replied, "But we learned from Pascal that life comes from life, so how can it come from non-life?"

The teacher said, "There was a moment in which various gases got together in proper formation, in the right combination, and in perfect timing. A flash of lightning struck, and life came into existence!"

"This is amazing! Are you saying there are situations in which all the right elements come together by chance, and then lightning strikes at the right moment? Are we talking about earth or outer space? Is there lightning in outer space? Moreover, lightning normally kills life, not create life!" The class discussion got more and more ridiculous.

Yet evolution has affected us to one degree or another, at the very least by planting a question mark into our minds. So whenever we think of creation, evolution would insert a question mark into our minds. Even if we don't believe in evolution, it has created a certain spiritual blindness that hinders us from seeing God's glory in creation. That is why we need to ask God to open our eyes.

2. God is revealed through the life and teaching of Christ

We come to the second line of evidence for God's reality. Jesus Christ is *par excellence* the one who reveals God's glory and nature. You may say, "That's fine, but I wasn't around when Jesus walked on earth. I'm not as privileged as the disciples who saw Jesus."

God came into the world by dwelling in the man Jesus, but God was at the same time veiled by the flesh because the body of Jesus both revealed and concealed God. If God had revealed Himself to us directly, we would die instantly because no one can see His face and live (Ex.33:20). When God revealed Himself on Mount Sinai, the Israelites were so terrified that they begged that no further revelation of God be given them because they could not endure His awesome presence. Yet at Sinai, God hadn't even revealed His full divine glory.

It is not only the person of Jesus but also his teaching that reveals and conceals at the same time. In Mark's gospel we find what is called the "Messianic secret," a term used by New Testament scholars to refer to the fact that Jesus, in his public teaching, does not explicitly reveal himself to be the Messiah, the Savior King. There is no utterance in his public teaching that explicitly says, "I am the Messiah". In Mark's gospel, only once does Jesus specifically say that he is the Christ, but that is only because the High Priest had commanded him to say under oath, during the judicial hearings in the Sanhedrin, whether he is the Christ, the One appointed by God to be the Savior of the world (this is the meaning of "Christ"). In Mark 14:61-62 and its parallel in Matthew 26:63-64, it is only in this special situation, and only under oath, that Jesus specifically says, "I am [the Messiah]."

We are to commit to Yahweh, who is God, and to Jesus Christ, the Son of God. But in the gospels, Jesus doesn't explicitly state who he is. If he doesn't even tell his disciples who he is, how can he expect us to know who he is? Jesus asks his disciples, "Who do people say that the Son of Man is?" (Mt.16:13) The disciples tell him that some say he is John the Baptist, some say Elijah, some say Jeremiah or some other prophet. Jesus doesn't tell his disciples who he is, yet he expects them to answer his question. Then Peter says, "You are the Christ, the Son of the living God." Jesus says to him, "Blessed are you Simon Bar-Jonah, for flesh and blood has not revealed this to you, but my Father who is in heaven" (Mt.16:17). Flesh and blood includes Jesus himself.

This brings us to the heart of commitment. Even if I could, I would not talk you into commitment, for then your faith would be based on human wisdom and the power of persuasion, and not on God's wisdom. Jesus never tries to persuade his disciples that he is the Christ, but leaves it to God to open their eyes. Commitment cannot be based on persuasion by "flesh and blood," a term that in Scripture refers to a human being.

Every committed person is a miracle of God's revelation. I marvel at God's work in every true Christian. You become a Christian only after God has revealed Himself to you, through Christ, in a way that no one else can. What I am doing in this discussion is to lay the groundwork for God to reveal Himself to you. Ultimately all commitment is of God's work, not man's. It also depends on how open you are to Him.

3. God is revealed through the cross

The third way in which God is revealed to us is through the cross of His Son Jesus Christ. God is revealed through His Son but nowhere more powerfully than at the cross. Anyone who looks at the cross of Christ and not see God's love and saving power will not be persuaded by any amount of talk. Good overcomes evil, and there is no greater example of this than at the cross of Jesus Christ.

Every Christian who is committed to God is a living testimony of God's good overcoming evil. As we saw in Colossians, all this is made possible by the cross. We need to meditate on the cross and ask God to show us what truly happened there, for no human eloquence can ever explain it to us.

One day when we see Jesus Christ the Son of God face to face, we will see him not merely as one with a crown that radiates His Father's glory, but as one with deep scars on his head etched by the crown of thorns. When he lifts his hands or when we fall at his feet, we will see the nail wounds. When he exposes his heart, we will be reminded that a Roman soldier used a lance to pierce through his side and into his heart such that blood and water came out. His scars will be there for all eternity.

Revelation repeatedly speaks of Jesus as the Lamb that was slain. This Lamb of God will forever bear the scars of its violent death. God's glory is forever revealed in Jesus Christ, not merely as one who did miracles and other impressive feats on earth by God's power (Acts 2:22), but as one who died for us.

Paul says, "I decided to know nothing among you except Jesus Christ and him crucified" (1Cor.2:2). He also says, "May I never boast except in the cross of our Lord Jesus Christ, through which the world has been crucified to me, and I to the world" (Gal.6:14). Paul could have gloried in many things such as his Damascus Road encounter with Jesus or the many miracles he had done by God's power, yet he doesn't want to talk about them, for he only wants to talk about the cross of Jesus Christ.

Do you see God's glory in the cross of His Son Jesus Christ? Probably not, for the cross reveals and conceals. The glory of the cross is hidden by the shame of the cross, for Jesus died a criminal's death. Until we are willing to see the shame, we won't see God's glory and reality at the cross of His Son Jesus Christ.

4. God is revealed through the resurrection

The fourth way in which God is revealed to us is the resurrection of His Son. Ponder on the empty tomb and what happened to the body of Jesus. His dead body was in the hands of the Roman soldiers who were under the supervision of a Roman officer and under the authority of Pilate, the Roman governor. So where did the body go? The Romans only had to produce the body to disprove any claim of the resurrection of Jesus. It was the Romans, not the disciples, who were in possession of Jesus' body.

The enemies of Jesus were fully aware that while he was alive, he spoke publicly and repeatedly of his resurrection from the dead. Hence it would have been stupid of his enemies if they had allowed his body to leave their sight for even one minute. And did they make that elementary mistake? Not according to the records that we have. It was in the vested interests of the Jewish leaders and the Romans to avoid making that mistake. We are told that Jesus' tomb was formally sealed by the Roman officials and guarded by Roman soldiers. Yet they could not produce his body when the disciples went about proclaiming the risen Christ. All that the authorities had to do was to display the body of Jesus in public.

Jesus was a public figure in Jerusalem, Judea, Galilee, and even in the temple. He stood before Pilate, before Herod, before the high priest, and before the multitudes. Everyone recognized his face, so the authorities only had to produce his dead body to disprove the claim of his resurrection. At the same time, because Jesus was widely recognized, it was impossible for his enemies to present another person's body as his body.

Moreover, the disciples didn't immediately run off to distant cities to proclaim the resurrected Jesus to people who wouldn't be able to confirm the claim. Instead the disciples remained in Jerusalem. At Pentecost, Peter spoke about "the resurrection of the Christ" to the same people who had crucified him (Acts 2:24,31,36).

All in all, when we look at the facts of Jesus' resurrection, we see the clear evidence that God is real.

5. God is revealed in the witness of the apostles

The fifth line of evidence of God's reality is the witness of the apostles who had seen the resurrected Jesus. In the New Testament, the word "apostle" is not limited to the Twelve but is a broad term that includes those who had witnessed Jesus's life, ministry, and resurrection. The apostolic witness includes the apostle Paul himself:

> For I delivered to you as of first importance what I also received: that Christ died for our sins in accordance with the Scriptures, that he was buried, that he was raised on the third day in accordance with the Scriptures, and that he appeared to Cephas, then to the twelve. Then he appeared to more than five hundred brothers at one time, most of whom are still alive, though some have fallen asleep. Then he appeared to James, then to all the apostles. Last of all, as to one untimely born, he appeared also to me. For I am the least of the apostles, unworthy to be called an apostle, because I persecuted the church of God. (1Cor.15:3-9, ESV)

Witnesses are crucial to the legal proceedings of a court of law. Consider how many witnesses had seen Jesus after his resurrection: not only the 12 apostles but 500 men all at once. Under Jewish law, two or three witnesses are enough to establish a case, yet Paul speaks of 500 witnesses. He wrote his letter to the Corinthians some thirty years after Jesus' resurrection. Most of the 500 witnesses were still alive and available for cross examination, though some had "fallen asleep" (died).

Finally Paul says, "Last of all, as to one untimely born, he appeared also to me." His testimony of Jesus is convincing because of his former violent persecution of the church (Gal.1:13,23). Paul's testimony is that of a former enemy of Jesus and the church. The supportive testimony of a former enemy is more convincing than that of a longtime friend. When an enemy publicly declares, "I used to imprison and kill Christians, but now I am a follower of Jesus Christ who has revealed himself to me," that testimony is most powerful.

6. God is revealed in the living witnesses today

The sixth line of evidence of God's reality is the living witnesses today. You might say, "Paul knew of 500 witnesses of the resurrection, many of whom could be cross examined, but they are no longer around." But have you considered the many living witnesses of God today who have experienced God's reality, and who far outnumber the 500 witnesses in Paul's time? There are many people living today who can testify of God's reality in their lives. Every true Christian is a testimony to God, and there are many such people in this generation. Bookstores are full of autobiographies and testimonies of people who have written of their experiences of God. God is at work today, not just 2,000 years ago.

I count myself as a witness. My testimony, published as *How I Have Come to Know God*, is a witness to God's reality, yet it includes only a small fraction of what I have experienced. Do I have any reason to tell you false stories? Is there any reason to doubt the accuracy of my witness? Is someone paying me to fabricate these stories? No, I am a living witness to God's reality. It would take me hours and hours to share what God has done in my life. The testimony of every Christian who has experienced God's reality ought to be taken seriously.

7. God is revealed in your life

The seventh line of witness is you yourself. Have you experienced God at all? When you look back at some of the events in your life, even those which you are not 100% sure that God was involved in, you can probably see that it was God who played a crucial role in your experiences.

H.D. Lewis, an eminent philosopher in England and one of the professors I sat under in London, once wrote a book, *Our Belief in God*, which was taken seriously because he was a respected philosopher. If the book had been written by someone else, perhaps no one would have taken serious notice of it. But because of Lewis's stature as a philosopher, people took notice of it and had to reckon with it.

In his book he reasons that there is a sense in which everyone, at one time or another, has had an experience of God, and this is the case whether you are a Christian or not. He gives an example from his own life as a non-Christian when he looked at the beauty of a sunset. He couldn't explain why, but he was sure that he was experiencing God in the sunset.

Some people have told me that they survived an accident that should have killed them. They couldn't understand why they were still alive. Did they experience an invisible protecting hand in the incident? And why are you reading this book about commitment to God? Is it because God has been guiding you in a way that is hidden and revealed at the same time?

This final line of evidence is ultimately you yourself. Ultimately the most convincing evidence of God's reality is what you yourself have experienced. This can be divided into two categories: what you experienced in the past, and what you can experience in the future.

Your past experiences

Some of the things you experienced in the past may be hazy in your memory yet are real all the same. My mother told me that when I was a baby, she came home one day and found me almost dead in my crib. A blanket had somehow wrapped tightly around me, suffocating me, and

I was turning blue. She hadn't been attending to me for some time, and if she had delayed a minute or two, I would have died. Was it a coincidence that she came home at the right moment? When she saw me, she had such a fright that she nearly fainted on the spot, which would have finished me off before she could regain consciousness. She had just enough presence of mind to unwrap the blanket, and so I am here alive today.

These are the sort of experiences that my professor was talking about. In one way or another, everyone has had a personal experience of God regarding which one could say, "I can't prove it, but God was involved." Look back at your own life and ponder on the things that may have been genuine experiences of God, even if you weren't aware of it at the time.

Jacob experienced this sort of thing when he wrestled with a person all night without knowing that he was wrestling with God (Gen.32:24-32). In another incident, in a dream Jacob saw a ladder extending from earth to heaven (Gen.28:11-22). He didn't know that God was present in the place where he was sleeping. He realized this only after waking up, and it gave him a fright. He had experienced God without knowing it until later.

Many of us have experienced God's kindness, mercy and protection without knowing it at the time. Maybe you thought it was pure luck or coincidence that a car hit the guy standing next to you and not you. Why did it happen that way? You might not have an answer, but you somehow know that God has an eternal plan for you.

Your future experiences

The second part of this line of evidence is what we can experience of God in the future. The whole point of this book is to inspire you with the hope of experiencing God's reality. You must experience God for yourself, for there is no way for me to prove God to you.

Jesus said to Martha, "Didn't I tell you that if you believe you would see God's glory?" (Jn.11:40) He said this to her after Lazarus, the brother of Martha and Mary, had died. Before Lazarus died, his sisters pleaded with Jesus to come save him but Jesus purposefully delayed his arrival until after Lazarus had died. It is important for us to realize that the Lord may allow something to happen that may look like a complete disaster, yet is meant to bring about something wonderful and glorious. Jesus waited until Lazarus had been dead four days. The mourners were crying their eyes out. They, especially Mary and Martha, were grieved that Jesus did not come in time to save Lazarus.

Jesus ordered the stone removed but Martha reminded him that Lazarus had been dead four days. His body would be decomposing and there would be a stench (v.39). Yet Jesus said to the dead man, "Lazarus, come out". He didn't say, "People, go in and carry him out." No one would have dared anyway. Instead he commanded Lazarus to come out by himself. The people were probably looking at each other and thinking that this was preposterous. Then Lazarus, all bandaged up, walked out of the tomb! It just boggles the mind.

Many want to see God's glory before they believe in Him, but the Bible reverses the order: First you believe and commit to God, then you will see His glory. But we like to reverse the order, asking God to reveal His glory first. This won't work because if you are unwilling to act on the evidence that is already before you, you won't receive any more.

The seven lines of evidence

Here are the seven lines of evidence we have looked at:

1. God's creation
2. The life and teaching of Jesus Christ
3. The cross
4. The resurrection
5. The witness of the apostles
6. The living witnesses today
7. Your own experience of God

If you reject these seven lines of evidence, you won't get any more, for it is on the basis of these that you are going to make your initial commitment. If these are not good enough for you, what is? God has given us enough evidence for us to make our commitment. He is not asking us to believe blindly. When you believe on the basis of the evidence before you, you will see God's glory. If the evidence is not good enough for you, no evidence will be enough.

In Montreal I once asked some people if they will believe that God is real if I should by God's power raise a dead person in front of their eyes as Jesus raised Lazarus. They said yes, they will believe and be committed. I said, "Then you haven't learned from history. Do you know how many people witnessed the raising of Lazarus? Do you think all of them committed their lives to God? If I raise a dead man right now, I guarantee you that many of you will not believe."

They asked why and I said, "Because we are skeptical by nature. Even if two or three doctors check a man's pulse and certify that he is dead, and if he is later raised from the dead, would you believe he was really dead in the first place? You normally don't doubt a death certificate but if someone raises a man who has been certified dead, you are going to doubt the competence of the doctors."

There are modern-day cases of people who have been raised from the dead, but does the world believe? No. What about the doctors who certified their deaths? Do they believe? If anyone should believe, surely it would be the doctors. But it is in human nature to find an argument to deny the reality of miracles even when it is nearly impossible to dismiss the evidence, either because the person has been dead for a time or because his skull is fractured. There are such cases today but do we believe them? Maybe with a question mark.

It is human nature to remain unconvinced by any evidence if one doesn't want to believe. But there is also the opposite danger of accepting any evidence, even weak evidence, at face value simply because we want to believe it. It is a problem with human nature that some are gullible enough to believe anything whereas others won't believe even the strongest evidence.

I hope you won't blindly believe everything that comes along your way. You need to be careful about miracles because they can be faked, so you are right to be skeptical of many of them. I have been to Lourdes in France where many have reportedly been healed of various diseases. At Lourdes there are memorials and offerings of gratitude set up by those who claim to have been healed. Are you skeptical? I believe that some of the healings are genuine and some are not. I will have to investigate the individual cases before determining to my satisfaction which are genuine and which are not. We have to be careful in this world. But we can also swing to the other extreme of being overly cautious such that no evidence speaks to us at all.

What evidence is convincing to you? God knows that I am a hard man to convince. I will examine and cross examine the evidence before I am satisfied that I have not overlooked anything. God knows that I am this kind of person. And do you know what? God welcomes that, provided you are willing to go to all lengths to examine the evidence. If you say, "I want to know the truth," God will be pleased to accept your challenge. But if you don't want to examine the evidence, God won't force you to.

What evidence of God's reality will convince me? I accept as evidence the fact that I didn't suffocate in the crib. But the evidence is both hidden and revealed. It is valuable to me only because God's reality is supported by other evidence. On its own, this incident would not convince me. I see God's hand in that incident only in retrospect, having experienced God in many other ways. Because I know that God is real for these other reasons, I can see that He did intervene to save my life. But without the additional supporting evidence, this incident alone would not convince me. I would dismiss as pure coincidence the fact that I didn't die. But because I know that God is real for other reasons, I don't see the incident as a coincidence.

What other past experiences are convincing to me? For one thing, my own transformation. What God can do with a man like me is convincing evidence to me. God's power that comes into my life and makes me a new person is something that no one, not even I myself, can achieve. We can change ourselves in terms of moral reform but we cannot transform ourselves into new people. We can quit smoking by sheer will power but it is beyond human ability to transform someone into a Christ-like person.

I used to have an explosive temper but God took it away. As I said, when you experience God's power in your life, you will know that He is real. When I was in school, I was known for being a person you couldn't fool around with. When my temper flared, it was a disaster for those around me. I was a sportsman in those days, strong and fit, and trained in the martial arts, and anyone who tangled with me was making a first-class mistake. Nowadays I am more of a pushover, as defenseless as a lamb. This transformation was not something I could do for myself, for I didn't even seek it. But God dealt with me in such a powerful way that He took away my temper. This experience is very convincing to me. You likewise have to experience God's transforming power to see how effective it is. This victorious transforming power is something I had experienced in the past but also continue to experience in the present. You have to experience God's power for yourself because it is not something I can convince you of.

If we open our hearts to the seven lines of evidence, we will begin to experience God's power. When we believe and commit to God on the basis of the evidence before us, we will be transformed. Is there any risk in allowing God to transform you? To my mind, the risk is zero. Medical doctors make mistakes because they are only human, but God makes no mistakes. If you go to Him as a patient with your problems and sicknesses, He will heal you. With God there is no risk for you, so what is your excuse for not going to Him? I am wary of getting hospital treatment because medical doctors are only human. They do their best but if they make one mistake, I might not come out alive. But there is no such risk with God. My question to all who are contemplating commitment: Are you willing to let God make you a new and good person?

When Christians don't live a committed life, what great blessings are denied them! They will spend the rest of their lives wondering if God is real. If you don't commit to God, you can never be sure of His reality, and God will keep it that way. I myself have no need to guess if God is real or not, for He grants His daily leading to those who are committed to Him. I hope that you will experience for yourself that God is real.

Part Two

Commitment to One Another

Loving One Another as Ourselves

Chapter 11

Lateral Love

What do we mean by "lateral love"? The word "lateral" can be a noun or an adjective. As an adjective it has to do with the sideward direction. In medicine, a lateral disease is one that affects one side or both sides of the body. In mechanics, a lateral force is one that acts at right angles to the direction of motion.

Similarly, lateral love is a love that is expressed in the horizontal direction, that is, among human beings. For the purposes of this book, it is specifically the brethrenly love among God's people. It is distinct from, yet related to, the vertical love between God and His people.

In the Bible, lateral love is not a minor topic but *the high point* of total commitment to God. Lateral love also happens to be that aspect of commitment that presents the greatest practical difficulties to most Christians. In Part Two of the present book, we now expound lateral love in five simple chapters.

The Kingdom of God

In discussing lateral love, we first need to realize that the kingdom of God is a central element in Jesus' teaching. This can be confirmed by looking up a Bible concordance or doing a computer search in a Bible program.

In Matthew's gospel, the kingdom is usually called "the kingdom of heaven"; in the other gospels, it is called "the kingdom of God" and never "the kingdom of heaven".[7] There is no difference in meaning between kingdom of God and kingdom of heaven (in fact the two refer to the same thing in Mt.19:23-24).

The kingdom of God means less a political or theopolitical entity, and more God's rule and reign. The kingdom of God is God's kingship, God's rule, and God's government in the lives of His people.[8]

Kingdom, kingship, rule, government—these words convey law and commands. In a kingdom or government, there is law, and law expresses itself in commands (cf. "the rule of law"). Contrary to what many Christians think, the New Testament has not abolished law and commands. Although we have finished with the Old Testament law, it doesn't mean that there is no more law. That is because we now come under a new law: the spiritual law.

Only one command

In fact the spiritual law was already present in the Old Covenant but is now given as a new command (1 John 2:7-8, NASB):

> Beloved, I am not writing a new commandment to you, but an old commandment which you have had from the beginning; the old commandment is the word which you have heard. On the other

---

[7] Matthew uses "kingdom of heaven" 32 times and "kingdom of God" 4 times (or 5 times, cf. manuscript variation in 6:33). By contrast, the rest of the New Testament uses "kingdom of God" 62 times and never "kingdom of heaven". The 62 occurrences are distributed as follows: Mark 14x, Luke 32x, John 2x, Acts 6x, Paul's letters 8x. These numbers do not include the shorter term "the kingdom" which is found in phrases such as "the gospel of the kingdom" (Mt.4:23) or "the sons of the kingdom" (8:12).

[8] The Greek word for "kingdom" (*basileia*) has the primary meaning of the kingship and royal rule of a king rather than the territory he rules over, though the latter sense is not excluded. The standard BDAG Greek-English lexicon gives two main definitions of this word: "(1) the act of ruling; a. *kingship, royal power, royal rule;* b. *the royal reign;* (2) territory ruled by a king, *kingdom.*" The sense of territory is listed as the second rather than the first definition, but more telling is the fact that BDAG gives ten times as many biblical and extra-biblical citations for the first definition (kingship and royal rule) than for the second definition (a king's territory).

hand, I am writing a new commandment to you, which is true in Him and in you, because the darkness is passing away and the true Light is already shining.

John's repeated mention of a new command or commandment mirrors Jesus' use of "command" to refer to one specific command: *love one another.* If you look up a concordance, you would see that when Jesus speaks of "command" in terms of the spiritual law, it refers to the command to love.[9] In John's writings, the command to love is the central element of the new covenant.

Something important and astonishing emerges from the fact that in the new covenant, one command sums up the kingdom of God. If we live under God's kingship, there is only one fundamental requirement for us to obey: *love one another.* As we shall see, this command brings in other aspects of the spiritual life such as self-denial or overcoming the flesh and its resistance to the command of love.

The kingdom of God, I repeat, has only one fundamental command: *love one another.* The Jews have counted 613 commands in the Hebrew Bible, with the Ten Commandments elaborated into many individual commands. But in the New Testament, the law is summed up in one command. This command is so fundamental that anyone who fails to live by it thereby declares that he or she is not living under God's kingship and is not in God's kingdom. To acknowledge God as King in your life and therefore to have a place in His kingdom on earth (which in the present age exists as the church), you must live by this command. It is not something optional.

We must not allow the familiarity of the words "love one another" blind us to their importance. It is Satan's tactic to make us tired of hearing familiar words such as "love one another" or "commit to God". Someone once told me, "The church is always talking about commitment and commitment, and I am sick of it." If you are tired of the word *commitment,* you have already fallen into Satan's trap.

---

[9] In the NT, "command" is used in one of two senses, either the OT commandments or the new law in God's kingdom summed up in love.

Three interconnected elements: kingdom, the Spirit, love

The Bible provides an unbroken link between the kingdom of God and the Holy Spirit (the Spirit of God). Where the Spirit is, there is the kingdom. Where there is not the Spirit, there is not the kingdom. Jesus brings this out when he says, "But if I cast out demons by the Spirit of God, then the kingdom of God has come upon you" (Mt.12:28). Paul expresses this from a different angle: "For the kingdom of God is not eating and drinking, but righteousness and peace and joy in the Holy Spirit" (Rom.14:17).

The link extends to a third element: Where the Spirit is, there is love. Hence there is a scriptural connection between three things: God's kingdom, God's Spirit, and God's love in us. The connection between the last two is seen in Rom.5:5 (God's love has been poured into our hearts by the Holy Spirit) and Gal.5:22 (the fruit of the Spirit is love).

This link between love and the Holy Spirit indicates that loving the neighbor is achieved not by human effort but by the Spirit's work in our hearts that empowers us to love as God loves. We know from experience that we cannot love our neighbor in our own strength, but it is possible by God's transforming work. God's project in the present age—that of establishing His kingdom on earth—is realized by the Spirit's work in us, creating a new community of God's people among whom there is love.

The connection between these three things—God's kingdom, God's Spirit, God's love—gives us a grand vision of the church. When we fulfill lateral love, there will be a community of such beauty that the world will marvel that God's people can love each other with the love of Christ.

In the church—which in the present age is the earthly manifestation of God's kingdom—spirituality is measured by one criterion: *lateral love*. According to Scripture, spirituality is gauged by whether one has self-giving love and not by things such as the power to do miracles, for miracles do not necessarily prove submission to God's kingdom. Many will plead, "Lord, Lord, did we not prophesy in your name, cast out demons in your name, and perform many miracles in your name?" but the Lord will say to them, "I never knew you; depart from me, you who practice lawlessness" (Mt.7:22-23). They are rejected as evildoers for failing to do God's will (v.21), including the command of lateral love.

No shortcut to spirituality

To repeat: In the New Testament, spirituality is gauged by only one thing: *lateral love*. Jesus speaks of lateral love when he says, "This I command you, that you love one another" (Jn.15:17). It is even made the basis of our friendship with Jesus: "You are my friends if you do what I command you" (v.14).

Many Christians use other criteria such as the speaking in tongues to gauge spirituality. They equate speaking in tongues with spirituality, but we must not fall for this nonsense. I have had to tell people who spoke in tongues that in their particular cases, they were unregenerate. Initially they were shocked but later realized that I was right.

I once watched a television report about some churches in southern United States that gauge spirituality by the ability to handle venomous snakes. They base this on Mark 16:18, "They will pick up snakes with their hands; and if they should drink deadly poison, they will not be harmed". The documentary shows people holding deadly snakes, even two or three at a time. In the past ten years, two persons among them had died from snake bites. One of them, a relative of a person who is still attending the church, was bitten by a copperhead; he died a slow and agonizing death over a period of 11 hours because he didn't allow the doctors to give him an antiserum. He said it was God's will for him to be bitten and therefore God's will for him to die.

The documentary shows a man consuming strychnine, a dangerous alkaloid used in rat poison. He drank a cup of water laced with an amount of strychnine that was, according to the documentary, enough to kill several adults. A scientist took some of the powder to a laboratory for analysis and confirmed that it was strychnine. Yet the one who drank the water wasn't harmed. So he must be spiritual, right? Well it proves nothing of the sort.

I stress again that in Scripture, spirituality is not gauged by things such as handling venomous snakes. In fact this is contrary to scriptural practice. When Paul was gathering firewood, a snake came out and bit him in the hand (Acts 28:3-6). The onlookers were expecting him to die but he shook off the snake and wasn't harmed. The key difference is that he wasn't looking for a snake to handle. Similarly, Mark 16:18 is not telling us to look for poison to drink, but that if you should some-how consume poison, God can protect you from its harmful effects.

Lateral love: Jonathan and David

The self-giving love between Jonathan and David is something that the church has admired through the ages. The pure and beautiful relation-ship between them is not meant to be a one-of-a-kind rarity but a model for the New Testament church:

> After David had finished talking with Saul, Jonathan became one in spirit with David, and he loved him as himself. (1Sam.18:1, NIV)

How did Jonathan love David? *As himself*. This brings to mind Jesus' command to "love one another as I have loved you" (Jn.15:12) and "you shall love your neighbor as yourself" (Mt.22:39). The words "as yourself" in the latter verse are explained by "as I have loved you" in the former.

The command is not just to love the neighbor but the neighbor *as yourself*. It is to love the neighbor as your own soul, just as Jonathan loved David as his own soul. We see this again in 1Sam.18:3: "Jonathan made a covenant with David because he loved him as himself". He was fulfilling the great command of love.

We will look into *as yourself* in the next chapter, but it is already clear that *as yourself* is exemplified in the love between Jonathan and David. Its importance is seen in the fact that the story of their relation-ship takes up four chapters (18,19,20,23) in First Samuel.

First-degree relationships, not second-degree

The New Testament speaks of love within the church that is characterized by first-degree relationships, not second-degree relationships. What do I mean by this? A first-degree relationship is the closest possible family relationship such as the parent-child relationship or the sibling relationship. On the other hand, the relationship between cousins is second or third degree, depending on relational distance. In the New Testament, there are no aunts, uncles, cousins, but there are brothers, sisters, fathers, mothers:

> Do not rebuke an older man, but exhort him as a father, younger men as brothers, older women as mothers, and with all propriety, the younger women as sisters. (1Tim.5:1-2, HCSB)

Paul speaks of first-degree relationships in the church, not second-degree. Does it mean that we start calling everyone Mother or Father and so on? Even if we are not ready for that, in our hearts we can still regard an older person as our mother or father, bridging any distance that may come between us.

I was amused when someone once told me he had a problem with an elderly woman who wanted him to call her "mother". The reason was that she was like a mother to his wife. Not a biological mother but more like a godmother, actually closer than a godmother. After the couple got married, the elderly woman wanted the husband to address her as mother. He refused and she was upset.

When he talked to me about it, I said, "Why not call her *mother*?" He said, "What!?" I said, "What's the problem? By all means call her *mother*. Isn't it good to have more than one mother?" He was stunned but said "okay."

In Mt.19:27, Peter asks the Lord Jesus, "We have left everything and followed you, what then will we have?" Jesus says that those who have left houses, brothers, sisters, father, mother, children, and land, will "receive a hundredfold and will inherit eternal life" (v.29). In applying the hundredfold increase to brothers, sisters, father, mother, children, Jesus is talking about the church family and not one's biological family.

In Mt.12:48 Jesus asks, "Who is my mother and who are my brothers?" He is not referring specifically to his mother Mary, for he goes on to say, "Whoever does the will of my Father in heaven is my brother and sister and mother".

Obstacles to lateral love

In the command of lateral love we see a beautiful picture of the church in which there are the closest possible relationships. All this is achieved by the power of the Spirit and the purity of a holy life.

Yet we set up obstacles to lateral love. We even use religious duty as an excuse, similar to what we see in the parable of the good Samaritan (Lk.10:25-37). Jesus gives this parable in answer to a scribe's question, "And who is my neighbor?"

In the parable, a man is attacked by robbers and left for dead on the road to Jericho. Along comes a priest, then a Levite, both of whom walk past the injured man without helping him. They even walk on the other side of the road to keep their distance from him. These religious leaders have religious duties to perform for God, and this prevents them from loving the neighbor. For if they stop to help the dying man, and if it turns out that he is dead, they would become unclean and unable to perform their religious duties to God.

They are prevented from helping the man because of the way they apply the law on touching a corpse (Lev.21:1,11; Num.19:11-13). The fear is that if the man is dead, then by touching him they would become ceremonially defiled. A priest who is defiled cannot serve in the temple, and the same for the Levite, so they don't want to take a risk in checking if the man is still alive. The fear of being defiled by a corpse prevents them from loving the neighbor.

But loving God and loving the neighbor cannot be separated. The priest and the Levite don't see the unity of the two commands, so they disregard the second in order to fulfill the first in terms of religious duty.

Christians similarly use Christian reasons for not loving the neighbor. For example, the allegiance to a certain doctrine, as they understand it, prevents them from fellowshipping with other Christians. We say that so-and-so is a Catholic or holds to a doctrine we don't agree with, so we erect barriers.

The word "heretic" is thrown around freely in the church today. There is a book with the interesting title, *Will the Real Heretics Please Stand Up? A New Look at Today's Evangelical Church in the Light of Early Christianity*, by David W. Bercot. This book says it is usually those who hold the right doctrines who are called heretics whereas those who hold the wrong doctrines are the ones who, sometimes out of insecurity, label others as heretics.

Our guiding principle ought to be the biblical truth and not the defense of a doctrine or theology. If you have the truth, I will submit to it. But you will have to prove your position from Scripture and be willing to subject it to cross-examination for the sake of arriving at the truth.

Love attests that we are his disciples

There is only one way for people to know that we are Jesus' disciples. It is not by our preaching, Bible knowledge, or good deeds done out of uncertain motives, but by our love for one another.

> A new commandment I give to you, that you love one another: *just as I have loved you, you also are to love one another.* By this all people will know that you are my disciples, if you have love for one another. (John 13:34-35, ESV, italics added)

In the italicized sentence, the absolute standard established in the first half ("just as I have loved you") sets the absolute standard for the second half ("you also are to love one another"). 1John 3:16 makes this concrete: "By this we know love, that he laid down his life for us, and we ought to lay down our lives for the brothers".

The supreme example of this is seen in Jesus Christ, the good shepherd who lays down his life for the sheep (John 10:11). But the hired hand abandons the sheep when he sees a wolf coming because he is concerned about his own wages and safety. He would never put his life on the line whereas the good shepherd who dies for the sheep will regard nothing as too precious for him to give up for the sake of their safety. Church leaders too must be ready to lay down their lives for the brothers and sisters.

The teacher-disciple relationship is characterized by absolute commitment as seen in Paul's care for the church: "I endure all things for the sake of the elect, that they also may obtain the salvation which is in Christ Jesus" (2Tim.2:10). Paul also says, "Death works in us, but life in you" (2Cor.4:12). This self-giving love is also intended for the marriage commitment, for husbands are to love their wives as Christ loved the church and gave himself up for her (Eph.5:25).

Loving God is loving your neighbor as yourself

> If anyone says, "I love God," and hates his brother, he is a liar; for he who does not love his brother whom he has seen cannot love God whom he has not seen. (1Jn.4:20, ESV)

In the past I have said lightheartedly—yet also seriously—that it is easy to love God because we don't see Him, but hard to love the brothers and sisters precisely because we see their faults. It's easier to love someone you don't see because you can idealize him or her. It's like hearing a warm and tender voice on a radio program that makes you imagine a nice and beautiful person. But when you get to see him or her in person, you may be in for a shock. You idealize those you don't see but it is hard to love your roommate whose faults are displayed right before your eyes.

In the verse just quoted, John is not playing around with words or platitudes. If you don't love your brother, the fact is that you don't love God. Any love for God with no corresponding love for His people is a fictional and idealized love that is unacceptable to God. To prove my love for Him, God requires me to love my brothers and sisters.

There are two fundamental reasons for this. The first is based on the fact of God's creation, for your brother or sister was created in the image of God. But today many Christians believe that God's image in man has been destroyed. If that were so, we would have lost one major reason for practicing lateral love. But in the Bible, God's image in man has not been destroyed. Note the present tense in "he is the image and glory of God" (1Cor.11:7; also Gen.9:6). Because a brother is in God's image, you are to love him despite his faults. You do this for God's sake because this brother bears God's image even if the image may appear marred or imperfect to you. You look beyond the imperfection and see a certain beauty in the person.

The other reason for lateral love is the redemption by which we have been incorporated into the body of Christ. Your brother or sister, despite his or her faults, is a member of the body of Christ. You cannot love Christ without loving the members of his body. Any love for Christ that does not have a love for his body is fictional and idealized.

Every metaphor of the church in the New Testament is a picture of mutual commitment. In the metaphor of the church as a body, there are no second-degree but only first-degree relationships. The only way to have second-degree relationships is to have a different body from the body of Christ. Another picture of the church is that of an army in which every soldier is committed to his fellow soldiers, for they need one another to survive. A soldier who goes off by himself will become an easy target for sniper fire. His survival depends on his belonging to an army whose members are committed to one another.

Sin destroys lateral commitment

Finally, sin is fundamentally a violation of your relationship with your neighbor, whether it is a sexual sin or a material sin such as stealing. Sin always causes spiritual injury to our neighbor. Even the sin of idolatry—which we usually regard as something done to God and not the neighbor—causes spiritual harm to your neighbor because your idolatry may stumble him.

But the one who loves his neighbor has fulfilled the law (Rom.13:8). Paul doesn't mention the first commandment but only the second as being sufficient for fulfilling the law. The first and second commands are inseparable; in fulfilling the second, you have fulfilled the first.

What will happen when there is no more lateral love in the church? There will be nothing left but an organization with a set of doctrines.

Nothing of value will remain in the church when there is no Jonathan-David love.

Chapter 12

As Yourself

In this chapter we look at "as yourself" in greater depth. These two words are taken from the well-known command, "You shall love your neighbor as yourself," a statement which occurs many times in the Old and New Testaments: Lev.19:18; Mt.19:19; 22:39; Mk.12:31; Lk.10:27; Rom.13:9; Gal.5:14; Jms.2:8; we can also include Lev.19:34.

The early church fathers are silent on "as yourself"

As I was pondering on the words "as yourself," I decided to consult the Ante-Nicene Fathers [10] to see what insight they might have on *as yourself.* To my surprise, I found no discussion on *as yourself* in the 10-volume Ante-Nicene Fathers.

There is similar silence on "as yourself" in the *Ancient Christian Commentary on Scripture* (ACCS), a 29-volume compilation of what the early church writers wrote on the Bible from Genesis to Revelation. The silence is remarkable because of the wide scope of ACCS, which covers not only the Ante-Nicene Fathers but also the Nicene and Post-Nicene Fathers, and even early heretics.

In ACCS, no early church writer even mentions "as yourself" for Lev.19:34; Mt.19:19; 22:39; Mk.12:31; James 2:8. These make up half of the verses listed in the beginning of this page. As for the other half of

---

[10] Prefix *ante* means "before". The Ante-Nicene Fathers are the early church fathers who lived before the Council of Nicaea which convened in AD 325.

the verses listed, "as yourself" is mentioned only in passing or with a one-sentence explanation:

- For Luke 10:27, ACCS has one mention of *as yourself*, but Ambrose simply quotes "your neighbor as yourself" without discussing it.

- For Galatians 5:14, ACCS has one mention of *as yourself*, but Victorinus simply quotes "your neighbor as yourself" without discussing it.

- For Leviticus 19:18, ACCS has one mention of "you shall love your neighbor as yourself," but Augustine inexplicably mis-reads this as "no one loves himself unless he loves God"!

- For Romans 13:9, ACCS has two mentions of *as yourself*. Chrysostom simply quotes "as yourself" without discussing it, whereas Pelagius says, "For one who loves his neighbor as himself not only does him no wrong but also does him good."

Hence, in the entire ACCS, the best that we can find for *as yourself* is a one-sentence explanation from Pelagius who is viewed by many in the church as a heretic. I am puzzled as to why something as important as "as yourself," which comes from the greatest commandments, is not given any discussion apart from a few passing references.[11]

I then searched through the modern commentaries but found no discussion on *as yourself* of any depth. Why are the commentaries ignoring the two key words taken from the greatest commandments? If I am commanded to love my neighbor as myself, isn't it crucial for me to understand what *as yourself* means? Why hasn't anyone in the past 2,000 years been tackling this most crucial question? The closest I have found on this subject is a work by Paul Ricoeur, a Catholic theologian

---

[11] Although ACCS is a 29-volume compilation, it is not exhaustive and may be missing a few references to *as yourself* by the early church fathers. But even if this were so, it probably would not alter the fact of the general silence on *as yourself*, for ACCS would likely include any commentary on *as yourself* that is weighty and significant.

and philosopher, but his book is written primarily as philosophy and not theology, and it is unclear in the end just how much of his book has to do with the scriptural idea.

One would think that the exegete—whose main task is to expound the word of God—would have as his highest priority a clear explanation of "love your neighbor as yourself" in order to help those who seek to live by the word of God. Perhaps the malaise of the church is that it doesn't seriously seek to live by the word of God.

The aim of this chapter

It is impossible to fully analyze *as yourself* in one chapter. My aim in this chapter is to get our minds started on the subject and to begin an initial exploration into the meaning of *as yourself*.

The statement "love your neighbor as yourself" originates in the Old Testament, in Lev.19:18, but we will examine it as it appears in the New Testament. The statement "love your neighbor as yourself" occurs 7 times in the New Testament: Mt.19:19; 22:39; Mk.12:31; Lk.10:27; Rom.13:9; Gal.5:14; Jms.2:8. We include as the eighth occurrence the minor variation in Mk.12:33 ("to love one's neighbor as oneself"). But we will skip Mt.22:39 because it is parallel to Mk.12:31, leaving us with seven verses to study. We now consider the seven verses, proceeding in biblical (canonical) order.

Occurrence #1: "As yourself" and possessions

The first instance of "love your neighbor as yourself" is found in Matthew 19:19, spoken by Jesus to the rich young ruler. Their discussion centers on eternal life and was in fact started by the question, "Teacher, what good deed must I do to gain eternal life?" (v.16). Hence "love your neighbor as yourself" is connected to eternal life in some way.

The young ruler says he has kept the commandments (v.20), including that of loving the neighbor as oneself (v.19). Jesus then brings in the matter of *perfection* in order to give concrete meaning to "love your neighbor as yourself". Hence he says to the rich young ruler, "If you want to be perfect, go, sell your possessions and give to the poor" (v.21). In order for the rich young ruler to love his neighbor as himself, he has to sell all his possessions and give to the poor.

In speaking of loving your neighbor as yourself, Jesus doesn't even cite Deuteronomy 6:5 of the Shema regarding loving the LORD your God with all your heart, all your soul, all your strength. Jesus doesn't quote the first command (love God with all your heart) but only the second command (love your neighbor as yourself) because the second includes the first. In fulfilling the second, one has fulfilled the first.

Occurrences #2 and #3: "As yourself" and a living sacrifice

We skip Mt.22:39 since it is parallel to Mk.12:31. Not counting this omission, the second and third occurrences of "love your neighbor as yourself" are found in Mark 12:31-33 (see the italicized statements):

> [31] "The second is this: *'Love your neighbor as yourself.'* There is no commandment greater than these." [32] "Well said, teacher," the man replied. "You are right in saying that God is one and there is no other but him. [33] To love him with all your heart, with all your understanding and with all your strength, and to *love your neighbor as yourself* is more important than all burnt offerings and sacrifices." (Mk.12:31-33, NIV)

Here we see two instances of "love your neighbor as yourself": the first is spoken by Jesus in v.31, the second is spoken by the scribe in v.33. The scribe makes the additional comment that fulfilling the command of love is more important than "all" the temple sacrifices put together. Coming from a Jew, that statement is most astonishing. Why are the temple sacrifices nothing compared to obeying the two great commands? Because if you love God with your whole being and your neighbor as yourself, you are a self-giving living sacrifice (Rom.12:1-2) which is far greater than the temple sacrifices. This is expressed concretely in Paul's statement, "They gave themselves first to the Lord and then to us in keeping with God's will." (2Cor.8:5)

Occurrence #4: "As yourself" and compassion and mercy

The fourth occurrence of "love your neighbor as yourself" is in Luke 10:27, a verse that leads up to the parable of the good Samaritan. Since we will be looking at this parable in the next chapter, I will make only one comment on how it explains loving your neighbor as yourself.

The Samaritan's deed in v.33 ("had compassion on him") depicts "love your neighbor" in terms of compassion. Similarly, v.37 ("showed him mercy") depicts "love your neighbor" in terms of mercy. Hence loving your neighbor involves compassion and mercy, which are God's own qualities. To love your neighbor as yourself is to become like God in His compassion.

Occurrence #5: "As yourself" and the fulfillment of the law

The fifth occurrence of "love your neighbor as yourself" is in Romans 13:9. We quote verses 9 and 10:

> The commandments, "You shall not commit adultery, You shall not murder, You shall not steal, You shall not covet," and any other commandment, are summed up in this word: "You shall love your neighbor as yourself." Love does no wrong to a neighbor; therefore love is the fulfilling of the law. (Rom.13:9-10, ESV)

In the last sentence we see the crucial fact that loving your neighbor as yourself fulfills the whole law. Because the second command (love your neighbor) fulfills the law, Paul doesn't even mention the first command (love God). As in Mt.19:19, the second command includes the first, so Paul is simply teaching what Jesus teaches.

Although the first and second commands are identical in many respects, they are not equal. Loving the neighbor is not exactly the same as loving God, otherwise we may think that we can spend one hour talking with our neighbor in place of spending one hour with God in prayer.

Occurrence #6: "As yourself" and serving one another

The sixth occurrence of "love your neighbor as yourself" is in Galatians 5:14. We quote verses 13 to 15:

> For you were called to freedom, brothers. Only do not use your freedom as an opportunity for the flesh, but through love serve one another. For the whole law is fulfilled in one word: "You shall love your neighbor as yourself." But if you bite and devour one another, watch out that you are not consumed by one another. (Gal.5:13-15, ESV)

Again the whole law is summed up in one command: you shall love your neighbor as yourself. Paul makes this a parallel to "through love serve one another": to love your neighbor is to serve your neighbor through love. Paul allows no middle ground: you either serve one another or "bite and devour" one another.

Occurrence #7: "As yourself" and the royal law

The seventh and final occurrence of "love your neighbor as yourself" is in James 2:8: "If you really keep the royal law found in Scripture, 'Love your neighbor as yourself,' you are doing right." (NIV)

We have discussed the link between the kingdom of God and God's love in us. James 2:8 includes these two things in what is called "the royal law," a term that can also be rendered "the law of the King". This royal law is none other than the command to "love your neighbor as yourself." The next verse (v.9) tells us not to show favoritism, which means that everyone is equal under the law of love.

These are the seven instances of "love your neighbor as yourself" in the New Testament (not counting Mt.22:39 which is parallel to Mk.12:31). Scripture doesn't simply say *love your neighbor* but raises the standard to *as yourself*. It is treating the other person as if he or she were yourself. It must mean at least that much.

But how do you treat the other person as yourself if he doesn't look like you or dress like you? He may belong to a different age group, or come from a different culture, or has a different hairstyle. How is it possible for me to treat him as myself or as an extension of myself? Should I regard him as my *alter ego* (Latin for "other me")—a person like me, yet not me?

The end of yourself

Let's now look at the real-life challenges of *as yourself*. At the very least, it must mean tearing down the barriers to communication and mutual understanding, otherwise I wouldn't be able to think of you as myself. That would be the case if you are a woman and I am a man, or you come from Mexico and I come from Madagascar: I can't think of you as myself because I don't know what it's like to be you. I have to pull down the barriers that stand between us, and understand what it is like to be you. This is an amazing exercise in which I sit back, look at you, and ask myself, "What is it like to be you? How would I think if I were you?" To think like you, I would have to stop thinking my thoughts. The words "as myself" would mean the end of myself.

A barrier gives protection, so if I pull it down, I would be defenseless. The barrier safeguards my security and individuality, so pulling it down and accepting you as myself would undermine that security. There is no more "me" when that "me" has become "you".

In every direction you turn, you will encounter a barrier between you and others. Even if you are willing to pull it down, others may not: "Keep your distance from me. If you become me, what will happen to me?" They feel that you are threatening their "me". But if both sides have no more "me," then the barriers are removed on both sides.

But there is a potential complication: Some people express love in a controlling way. They take over every aspect of your life, even telling you what you may eat. This kind of love is terrifying because it is possessive and seeks to control. To this kind of love we say, "No thanks. Keep your love to yourself and I will keep mine to myself. Then we'll all be happy."

Jesus never says that loving the neighbor means to take over his life as if it were mine. Am I giving or taking? If I take possession of your life as if it were mine, I would be loving you as myself but not in the way God intends. Maybe you don't even want me. It is like rejecting a marriage proposal where one says, "I am giving myself to you!" but the other says, "No thanks, you keep to yourself. I'm happy with myself."

Another problem is that we don't always love ourselves in the right way. To give a down-to-earth example, some people eat so much sweets that they become obese and lose their teeth. If they love you as themselves, they will stuff you with the foods that will ruin your health.

I won't examine *as yourself* fully in this chapter. I only want to give you an idea of how deep and complex the issues are. One thing does come out: To tear down the barrier between myself and someone else, I must be willing to die. Tearing down the barrier signifies my death as an individual because I am giving up my rights and what is important to me. These I sacrifice in order to establish a harmony in which the other person stands equal to me, not in terms of the law (under which all are equal) but such that your concerns and interests become my concerns and interests.

Humanly we can do this to some extent, but not in the full sense in which every interest of yours becomes mine. This is humanly unattainable, even humanly unacceptable, because your interests might not align with mine. To fulfill this command, I would have to learn what your interests are and what values are dear to you, and make them my own. This is almost unattainable even in a marriage.

In analyzing *as yourself*, we are simply using the language of love. Jonathan loved David as himself and gave him everything, even his own armor and throne. Love does that sort of thing, for the love of neighbor means the death of the self, the total denial of the self.

Here we see the vast difference between "love your neighbor" and "love your neighbor as yourself". The first can be done with limited love. If someone needs two dollars, we give him two dollars. If he needs a hundred, we give him a hundred, if we can afford it. But "love your neighbor as yourself" has no limits and requires total self-denial. This is related to Jesus' teaching about taking up the cross and denying oneself.

Loving the neighbor with limits is not what Jesus taught. We may have obeyed the command to love the neighbor, but not *as ourselves*. If you cook a meal or wash the dishes for your housemates when you are tired, you are showing them love even if there may be mild resentment in your heart. But if you love your neighbor *as yourself*, can there be any resentment? There can't be because the deed was done to *yourself*. The resentfulness arose because you did not regard the other *as yourself*. There is a qualitative difference between loving the neighbor and loving the neighbor as yourself. The words *as yourself* change the nature of the command.

Even more than yourself

But it doesn't stop there, for it turns out that loving the neighbor as yourself means loving the neighbor even more than yourself!

Let's say I have two bowls of rice and you have none. We are both hungry. My two bowls are just fine for me but because you are hungry, I give you one bowl. You now have one bowl, I have one. That is equality and a practical fulfillment of *as yourself*. My stomach yearns for two bowls, but because I love you as myself, we have one bowl each.

Suppose I have two jackets and you have none. It is wintery cold, so I need both jackets to keep warm. But you are shivering, so I give you one of my jackets. We both shiver a bit but not severely.

But if I have one jacket and you have none, how do I love you as myself? Do I tear the jacket in half so that each has half? If I do that, neither of us will have a jacket. To love you as myself, I give you the whole jacket and I have none. To love you as myself, I love you more than myself.

Sharing jackets is not a big issue compared to some real-life situations. If only one of us could get out of a situation alive, how do I love you as myself? If I save my life, you will die. So I choose to die so that you may live. To love you as myself, I love you more than myself.

In 1993, a barge floating down a river in Alabama struck a bridge. A short while later, an Amtrak train reached the bridge and derailed into the river. On board were a couple and their eleven-year-old daughter who was paralyzed and confined to a wheelchair because of cerebral palsy. When the train plunged into the river and water was rushing in, the parents' first thought was to save their daughter who was helpless to save herself. They struggled together to push her out the window with help from the rescuers. In the end, the girl survived but the parents died. They could not save themselves just as it was said of Jesus at the cross, "He saved others but cannot save himself".

In loving the child as themselves, the parents loved her more than themselves. Some may ask if the sacrifice was worth it. Aren't two healthy adults worth more than one disabled child? But that question never crossed their minds. Love makes no such calculations. Love does not measure a person's worth by her ability to contribute materially to society. If the parents had saved themselves, perhaps they could have had another child, one who is healthy. But that kind of cold calculation is the denial of love. In the choice between saving yourself and saving another person, you end up with the remarkable outcome that loving your neighbor as yourself means loving him or her more than yourself. The term *as yourself* is not an equal sign but a greater-than sign, in that you regard the other person's welfare as being more important than your own.

How much do we love ourselves?

Let's reverse our analysis: How much do we love ourselves? Let's be frank about it. If anyone does not love or take care of himself, something must be wrong with him. The truth is that we love ourselves. How hard do you work for your salary? Or study for your grades? We love ourselves with all our hearts, all our souls, all our minds, all our strength! Who else do we love as much as ourselves? No one even comes close. We love mom and dad if they don't get into our way. We love our friends if they don't irritate us, and the same with husband or wife. In the end, we love ourselves with our whole being.

The great command is functionally like this: You shall love the Lord your God with all the love you give *yourself*. The two great commands are saying the same thing: You shall love Yahweh your God as yourself, and your neighbor as yourself. These are the two sides of the equation.

Hence the second command is sometimes mentioned without mentioning the first.

Love takes mountain-moving faith

If the command was simply *you shall love your neighbor*, it is already hard enough. But to love your neighbor *as yourself* is impossible to the carnal man. It is hard even to love the one we have chosen to love. You presumably chose the person you are married to. You looked into the crowd and there stood this wonderful masculine person you fell in love with. Or you saw this ideal feminine representation of humanity. But after you get married, you discover it is hard to love the one you have chosen, never mind the rest of humanity.

It is humanly impossible to love your neighbor *as yourself*. To do this, mountains will have to be moved. The first mountain is the one inside us which elevates us to a height from which we look down on the rest of humanity. But when that mountain is removed, we will be brought down to the level of everyone else, and everyone will become *as myself*. The second mountain is the corresponding mountain in the other person. Given such insurmountable barriers, we soon realize that it is only by faith that such mountains can be removed. Jesus says in Mt.21:21 (cf. Mk.11:22-23):

> If you have faith and do not doubt, you will not only do what was done to the fig tree, but even if you tell this mountain, "Be lifted up and thrown into the sea," it will be done. (Mt.21:21, HCSB)

Salvation is by grace through faith, not by works. By this grace, God's transforming power enables us to fulfill His commands. Let's imagine what will happen if everyone, by faith, fulfills the command of love. This will lay the foundation of a glorious vision. In this age, can we envisage a community of people who love the neighbor *as oneself*, where everyone is *as oneself* such that there is *one self* shared among all? I hope I have fired up your imagination so that you can see, on the one hand, the depth of the Lord's teaching, but also see on the other hand the vision before us—a vision impossible to man but possible with God—of a community of people who live in love. It doesn't have to be a big community, for it takes only a small community of people who live by this command to shake the world by God's power!

If you examine the Old Testament's use of the word *neighbor*, you will see that it refers primarily, often exclusively, to the community of God's people. I think the rabbis have arrived at the same conclusion. It doesn't mean that we don't love those outside the community. Paul makes a distinction between the two: "Let us do good to all people and especially to those who are of the household of faith" (Gal.6:10). The universal love for humankind, including your enemies, is not on the same standing as love for God's people. A disciple of Jesus will love all people, even his enemies, but not equally. Your love for your enemy is not on the same level as your love for your brothers and sisters.

To achieve the goal of a community united by lateral love, we start by loving those close to us. Next we love those in the church whom we are not close to. Then we extend our love to God's people outside our churches. Then we extend our circle to include non-Christians, and finally, if we can manage it, those who are hostile to us.

But we must do this wisely, step by step. In athletic competition, you don't jump from the beginner's level to world-class competition in one step. You go step by step until you are ready to compete for the gold medal. In carrying out scriptural teaching, realism is important, for we could easily get lost in idealism. It is good to have ideals, but we must also be down to earth in fulfilling them.

Closing remark: Some non-Christians exceed Christians in the quality of their character, and that puts us to shame. Some non-Christians are not only willing to risk their lives to save others, they sometimes lose their lives in so doing. Many firemen have been killed in rescue efforts, notably those in the 9/11 attacks, some of whom were non-Christians. All over the world, there are policemen who die to save people. You may say that they're just doing their job, but the fact is that they have chosen that job of their own free choice, and actually put their lives on the line for the safety of others. These people seem to come under Romans 2:14: "when Gentiles who do not have the Law do instinctively the things of the Law" (NASB). We don't need to be dogmatic about the meaning of this verse. I think that Scripture, in God's wisdom, doesn't always allow us to arrange things in neat dogmatic categories.

True and self-giving love requires God's grace, but it seems that in Paul's teaching, that grace is sometimes made available to non-Christians. This may upset our neat theological categories but anyone who has worked with theology would know that God doesn't care about our neat categories. If something doesn't fit our categories, we tend to skirt around it. Some Christians say that the good works of non-Christians don't count whereas those of Christians count. This assertion casts doubt on God's fairness. If a non-Christian fireman dies in rescuing a stranger, his sacrifice means a lot to me and certainly more so to God. God's love is higher than our narrow-minded thinking.

Chapter 13

Who is my Neighbor?

Revitalized by God's word to become rivers of living water

We begin with a solemn warning by the Lord Jesus in John 12:48:

> The one who rejects me and does not receive my words has a judge; the word that I have spoken will judge him on the last day. (ESV)

Jesus personifies his word into an independent entity that will judge us on the last day. We will be judged by whether we have obeyed the word he has spoken. More generally we need to take heed in regard to any Bible teaching we receive, for we will be measured by it, to see if our lives come close to what we have been taught. It is a dangerous thing to keep on listening to the Bible and not practice it.

On the positive side, if God's word sparks a vision that blazes in our hearts, we won't need to spend our whole lives worrying about whether we are fulfilling it. That is because we will be powerfully motivated to carry out the word, not from any fear of judgment but because God's vision has taken root in our hearts. This positive, energized and forward-looking spirit is captured in Isaiah 42:9:

> The past events have indeed happened. Now I declare new events; I announce them to you before they occur. (HCSB)

God announces that new events will be coming. Yet at the same time we know that there is nothing new under the sun (Ecc.1:9) and that history repeats itself. While this is true in the human sphere, God now declares that new things will come. Indeed the next verse says, "Sing a new song to the LORD" (Isa.42:10). The newness and vibrancy of the spiritual life is captured one chapter later:

> [19] Look, I am about to do something new; even now it is coming. Do you not see it? Indeed, I will make a way in the wilderness, *rivers in the desert*. [20] The animals of the field will honor Me, jackals and ostriches, because I provide water in the wilderness, and *rivers in the desert*, to give drink to My chosen people. [21] The people I formed for Myself will declare My praise. (Isaiah 43:19-21, HCSB)

Verse 19 speaks of "rivers in the desert" as does verse 20. What is special about these rivers? Just as rivers in the desert give water to jackals and ostriches, so spiritual rivers in the spiritual desert "give drink to My chosen people" (v.20), namely, God's people whom He had formed to declare His praise (v.21). This brings to mind what Jesus says about the Spirit: "Whoever believes in me, as the Scripture has said, out of his innermost being will flow rivers of living water." (Jn.7:38) Rivers of living water in the spiritual desert! God's people will praise Him, for they will drink from the rivers in the desert, and become rivers of living water by the Spirit.

True assurance is based on love for God's people

The spiritual newness points to the new life. The true Christian is one who has passed from death to life, and loves the brethren:

> We know that we have passed out of death into life, because we love the brethren. He who does not love abides in death. (1Jn.3:14)

Love for the brethren is the way to know that we are saved and have passed from death to life. This is the biblical basis of assurance. Beware of any teaching of assurance such as "once saved, always saved" that bases the assurance of salvation not on obedience to God's word but on a verbal or intellectual profession of faith. Many have been led into thinking that we are saved merely by saying "I believe in Jesus" even if our lives fail to measure up to what God requires. There is nothing wrong in seeking assurance but we must distinguish true from false assurance. We know that we have passed from death to life if we love the brethren.

We previously saw the distinction between limited and unlimited love. We can love our neighbor in a limited way, say, by giving him two dollars, but the scriptural requirement is *as yourself*, which is unlimited love. We pass from death to life not because we have given two dollars to our neighbor, but because we love him as ourselves.

Two verses later John says, "We ought to lay down our lives for the brethren" (1Jn.3:16). Scripture gives us no option but to lay down our lives for the brethren. The word "ought" conveys a moral imperative but we ignore it because it threatens our very self.

When we read these two verses, v.14 and v.16, in combination, we arrive at the result that we pass from death to life if we love the brethren as ourselves, even to the point of laying down our lives for them.

Sandwiched in between these two verses is v.15 which says, "Everyone who hates his brother is a murderer." Note the strong word *hates*. The Bible is eminently practical; it doesn't give lofty ideals that are admired from a distance but are not carried out. Since proper exegesis requires us to interpret verse 15 with verse 14, we arrive at the important principle that *hate is simply the failure to love*. The Bible doesn't define hate as an intense dislike but simply as the failure to love. This Johannine definition is different from the usual understanding of hate as intense antipathy. In Scripture, the one does not love already abides in death, and the one who hates his brother is a murderer.

John's statement may sound radical but there is a practical reason for it. In a love relationship, there is a deep sensitivity to the other person. Anyone who has been in love would know this. Take the case of someone you don't love: If someone you don't love says something rude to you, you get irritated, but you brush it off because he or she means nothing to you. But if someone you love says an unkind word to you, it will stab your heart like a knife.

Instead of strengthening a relationship, we often wreck it with careless words and actions. The deepest relationship problems are often those in a marriage precisely because love is involved. One careless word causes hurt feelings. If all your enemies unite together to speak evil of you, that wouldn't hurt half as much as one unkind word from your spouse. Husbands and wives often don't realize this until they are at the receiving end of the insensitivity. We take the liberty to be rude to those familiar to us, but this will destroy the relationship in the end.

I used to wonder if the Lord Jesus was exaggerating in Mt.5:22, but when I understood his teaching better, I realized that he was not:

> But I tell you that anyone who is angry with his brother will be subject to judgment. Again, anyone who says to his brother, "Raca," is answerable to the Sanhedrin. But anyone who says, "You fool!" will be in danger of the fire of hell. (Mt.5:22, NIV)

When I first read this, I thought Jesus was exaggerating or speaking in hyperbole. Will we really face the highest council just for calling someone in church a fool or an idiot, especially if that seems to accurately describe someone who, in our view, has done something stupid or annoying? But Jesus says we will face the highest court. He is not talking about the courts in Israel because calling someone a fool is not punishable in the courts of Israel; he is talking about the spiritual tribunal before which we will stand. How many times have we said unkind words?

Anything that does not stem from love—any action or anger that negates love—will pave the way to a fearful judgment. That is because an action that does not stem from love kills. The failure to love already makes you a murderer. Your facial expression alone can hurt someone, for the one who sees it will wonder why you are angry with him. Maybe you were deep in thought, so you unintentionally walked past him without greeting him. The Lord is being practical when he says that we must not say anything, or do anything, or show any expression, that is not of love.

1John 3:19 says, "We shall know (by loving the brethren) that we are of the truth, and will assure our heart before Him." The assurance mentioned here continues on in verses 20 and 21, in the statement that "our heart does not condemn us". Many Christians seek the assurance of salvation, but the way to assurance is clear: obey the command to love, a command that is repeated again and again in 1 John.

Verse 22 goes on: "Whatever we ask we receive from him, because we keep his commandments and do what pleases him". If our prayers are not heard, it is because we are not living by this primary command of love. If we don't love our neighbor as ourselves or are unwilling to lay down our lives for the brethren, we can pray all we want, but God won't listen.

The parable of the good Samaritan: seven points

We now look further into "love your neighbor as yourself". We have seen that this teaching was fulfilled in the relationship of Jonathan and David; it is also meant to be fulfilled in the husband-wife relationship. Loving your wife is like loving yourself, for your spouse is an extension of yourself (Eph.5:28-29).

I now draw seven points from the parable of the good Samaritan which was given by Jesus in answer to a scribe's question, "And who is my neighbor?" The following is the whole parable and its context:

[25] On one occasion an expert in the law stood up to test Jesus. "Teacher," he asked, "what must I do to inherit eternal life?" [26] "What is written in the Law?" he replied. "How do you read it?" [27] He answered, "'Love the Lord your God with all your heart and with all your soul and with all your strength and with all your mind'; and, 'Love your neighbor as yourself.'" [28] "You have answered correctly," Jesus replied. "Do this and you will live." [29] But he wanted to justify himself, so he asked Jesus, "And who is my neighbor?"

[30] In reply Jesus said: "A man was going down from Jerusalem to Jericho, when he was attacked by robbers. They stripped him of his clothes, beat him and went away, leaving him half dead. [31] A priest happened to be going down the same road, and when he saw the man, he passed by on the other side. [32] So too, a Levite, when he came to the place and saw him, passed by on the other side. [33] But a Samaritan, as he traveled, came where the man was; and when he saw

him, he took pity on him. [34] He went to him and bandaged his wounds, pouring on oil and wine. Then he put the man on his own donkey, brought him to an inn and took care of him. [35] The next day he took out two denarii and gave them to the innkeeper. 'Look after him,' he said, 'and when I return, I will reimburse you for any extra expense you may have.' [36] Which of these three do you think was a neighbor to the man who fell into the hands of robbers?" [37] The expert in the law replied, "The one who had mercy on him." Jesus told him, "Go and do likewise." (Luke 10:25-37, NIV)

1. Seeking nothing in return

In a covenant relationship such as that between husband and wife or between Jonathan and David, there is a reciprocity in which I give myself to you, and you give yourself to me. But in the parable, the Samaritan shows absolute love to the injured man without thinking of reciprocity. It doesn't cross his mind to ask if the victim will return his love. It isn't even certain that he will survive, so reciprocity is irrelevant in the situation. In loving our neighbor as ourselves, *we seek nothing in return*, so that our motives for loving the neighbor may remain pure.

2. Not natural affection

The next thing we learn from the parable is that loving the neighbor is not based on natural affection. In the parable it is a Samaritan who helps an injured Jew. Samaritans have no natural affection for Jews. For many centuries they were despised by the Jews for various ethnic and religious reasons, and in turn they dislike the Jews. To love a Jew at all, the Samaritan has to overcome the insuperable obstacles in his own heart, including his natural dislike of Jews. There is nothing natural about loving your historic enemies.

3. Action rather than definition

The third point is that the meaning of *neighbor* is not a matter of definition. Typical of scholars and learned people, the scribe asks Jesus to define *neighbor* ("who is my neighbor?"). A common logical fallacy in philosophy is to think that we have arrived at an understanding of something just because we can define it. Arriving at a definition of *neighbor* doesn't mean that we understand what a neighbor is. In Scripture, understanding is tied to experience.

In fact Jesus refuses to answer the scribe's question with a definition. We like to play intellectual games with definitions: "If you are my neighbor, it logically follows that I am your neighbor. Since the relationship is commutative, I must love you, and you must love me." Even worse, we manipulate God's word to our advantage: "I am your neighbor, so you have to love me as yourself."

The Lord Jesus doesn't tell the scribe what a neighbor is, but *how to be a neighbor*. He turns nouns into verbs, and definitions into actions. At the end of the parable, he asks the scribe, "Who is neighbor to the injured man?" The scribe could only answer with a verb, "The one who showed him mercy" (v.37). The Lord rejects definitions that can be framed as nouns, but seeks actions that can be framed as verbs. He knows our hearts and how we juggle God's word to suit our purposes, even making ourselves the center of neighborly love.

4. A neighbor is a person in urgent need

The fourth point: In the parable, the question of how Jews historically view Samaritans is irrelevant because it is a Jew who needs help from a Samaritan. The question is meaningless even to the dying man because his life is at the mercy of a Samaritan. Perhaps more relevant is how Samaritans look at Jews, but even this question isn't going through the mind of the good Samaritan.

For him the urgent question is, "How can I help him? If I don't help him, he will die!" He can tell the victim's Jewish ethnicity by his clothes and appearance, but that is not important. His first concern is to treat his wounds and give him shelter for recovery. Jesus simply defines a neighbor as one who is in desperate need.

Jesus has a reason for using a Samaritan and a Jew as the main characters of the parable; it is so that we may see that natural affection plays no role in the definition of neighbor. *A neighbor is simply a person who is in need of love and care.* He is in desperation and his survival depends on someone else's mercy. He is poor in the sense of being helpless to help himself. He will surely die if he is left on the road. The striking thing is that his fellow Jews—a priest and a Levite—are willing to let him die, thinking that he is already dead or close to death.

5. The cost is total

This fifth point regarding total cost applies also to the rich young ruler (Mt.19:16-22). Many Christians reject the plain teaching of the story of the rich young ruler, as reflected in the often asked question: Is the requirement of selling all your possessions specific to the rich young ruler, or does it apply to Christians in general?

That we could even ask such a question shows that we have not understood the command of lateral love. Is the rich young ruler the only one who loves riches? Since he is hardly alone in loving riches, why would giving up one's possessions be specific to him? Are we saying that he loves riches more than anyone else? This cannot be proven exegetically. Moreover, Jesus says, "None of you can be my disciple who does not give up all his possessions" (Lk.14:33).

The rich young ruler is referring to the commandments, including that of loving the neighbor, when he says, "All these things I have kept. What do I still lack?" This shows that he doesn't truly understand the command of loving the neighbor. He thinks he has fulfilled it. But he is probably not being insincere when he says he loves the neighbor, at least in the way he understands it.

But Jesus sees only one way for the rich young ruler to fulfill the second command: Give all his possessions to his poor neighbors and become poor himself. At that time, most people in Israel were truly poor in the sense of abject material poverty, not "poor" by the standards of our modern world. In North America today, the poor can have fried chicken and ice cream, but in Jesus' day, the poor were truly poor as in the case of farmers who could not afford to have meat more than twice a year.

The rich young ruler says he has fulfilled the command of loving the neighbor. We are confident that he gives to charity as is required of every Jew. He would have given tithes to the temple. He would give to the poor, probably substantially, yet without hurting his wealth. He must have done all this or he wouldn't dare say he has fulfilled the commandments. He has fulfilled the moral teachings of the rabbis who taught the Jews to give to the poor, though not necessarily on the level of *as yourself.*

But the term *as yourself* changes the whole picture. The rich young ruler may have overlooked "as yourself" in Leviticus 19:18 but Jesus does not. He tells him that if he is to love the neighbor as himself, perfectly and absolutely, he must sell all his possessions and give to the poor. Then he will come down to their level and they will become an extension of himself. And who are the poor and needy? They are the sick, the widowed, the orphaned, and above all the spiritually destitute. This was our condition before we came to know God.

The fifth point of this parable, then, is that loving the neighbor as yourself will cost you everything.

6. Not judging the neighbor, but meeting his needs

The sixth point: Since our neighbor is one who is in need, our response to his need should not be based on feelings of natural love. We don't have to work up emotions to fulfill the command of love. In loving yourself, do you have to work up feelings for yourself? When you need something, you simply do what is needed to meet your need. Love is based on practical reality, not feelings. The key question is: Since my neighbor is in need, what can I do to take care of him? I don't need to have warm feelings towards him to help him.

Love does not judge. We must not judge according to our feelings for feelings are unreliable. We often don't know the true situation, so we shouldn't let our feelings run loose and ruin the atmosphere.

There is a true story of a person who was sitting in church. While the choir was singing, he focused his eyes on a particular choir member who was staring at the ceiling while singing, looking so smug and self-righteous. This annoyed the person who was watching him from the congregation. But when the service was over, he found out that the choir member was blind. So he felt ashamed that he had ruined his worship of God by a judgmental attitude towards a brother whom he thought was a hypocrite.

7. The power to love by the Spirit

It is clear by now that vast spiritual resources are required to love your neighbor as yourself. These resources are made available to us:

> "Whoever believes in me, as the Scripture has said, 'Out of his heart will flow rivers of living water.'" Now this he said about the Spirit, whom those who believed in him were to receive, for as yet the Spirit had not been given, because Jesus was not yet glorified. (John 7:38-39, ESV)

We often relate to people according to our feelings, so it is wonderful that the Holy Spirit is there to remind us not to judge. When the Spirit comes into our hearts, love flows again. God transforms us into people who function under the Spirit's control and are empowered to give of ourselves to others.

How glorious will be the church when its members give of themselves to one another, seeking nothing in return. We could start with a small group of people who are bonded together in covenant love. Then these few can expand into the core group of a vibrant church. This may seem like a dream but we have already seen that God can do marvelous things. He wants to do a new thing, namely, to create a new community that lives by the new covenant. We will strive with all the energy the Spirit inspires within us, to be not just hearers and declarers of the word, but also doers who live under the new covenant and bring into reality this new thing God has called into being.

Chapter 14

Commitment to be Led by the Spirit

W hen one becomes a Christian—a disciple of the Lord Jesus—he or she receives the Holy Spirit, the Spirit of God.[12] In this chapter we look at the work of the Spirit in our lives. This is of crucial importance because we cannot achieve anything of spiritual value in the Christian life apart from the Spirit. Salvation cannot be of works because what the Lord requires of us is beyond what we can achieve by human effort.

The Spirit's deep work at Pentecost

If every member of the church is totally committed to God, we will have a committed church. To see what are the marks of such a church, let us go back to Pentecost when the church began.

Pentecost had a powerful effect on the disciples. They were filled with the Spirit, and as a result they preached with boldness, prayed together, and spoke in tongues. The tongues spoken at Pentecost are not the same as the tongues that Paul describes in 1 Corinthians 12 to 14. The tongues at Pentecost were given for the purpose of proclaiming the word of God in the human languages understood by the visit-

---

[12] For the Holy Spirit as the Spirit of God: 1Cor.2:10-14; Gen.1:2; Ex.31:3; 35:31; Num.24:2; 1Sam.10:10; 11:6; 19:20,23; 2Chr.15:1; 24:20; Job 33:4; Eze.11:24; Mt.3:16; 12:28; Rom.8:9,14; 1Cor.3:16; 7:40; 12:3; Eph.4:30; Phil.3:3; 1Jn.4:2.

ors in Jerusalem (Acts 2:4-12). But the tongues in 1 Corinthians 14 are unintelligible to humans and don't edify anyone except the ones speaking the tongues. Hence Paul requires the interpretation of tongues if tongues are spoken in the church. But no interpretation was needed at Pentecost because the visitors could hear God's message in their own languages. The point of Pentecost was not the speaking in tongues as an end in itself but the gospel message proclaimed to the nations. The tongues were a channel to proclaim the good news of Jesus Christ to the multitudes gathered in Jerusalem. It was a temporary phenomenon because the visitors soon returned to their own countries.

The community of goods

The lasting result of the pouring of the Spirit at Pentecost was unity. Then something extraordinary came out of that unity: the community of goods, by which the people of the Jerusalem church shared all possessions in common.

First a caveat: The community of goods is a noble ideal but we must make sure it doesn't become a purely external arrangement. It is possible to give all your possessions and surrender your body to be burned, yet not have love (1Cor.13:3). The community of goods is meaningful only when everyone loves his neighbor as himself. At Pentecost this was fulfilled in the church by the work of the Spirit that empowered God's people to love their neighbor as themselves. Only then can there be the community of goods in its pure sense.

> They began selling their property and possessions, and were sharing them with all, as anyone might have need. (Acts 2:45, NASB)

This is a concrete expression of loving the neighbor as oneself. The people at Jerusalem saw each other as extensions of themselves: your need is my need, so I will give you what is mine to meet your need. This was achieved by the work of the Spirit because the community of goods in Jerusalem was not a passing fad but something that grew out of a deep sense of oneness. 1 John 3:17 says:

> But if anyone has the world's goods and sees his brother in need, yet closes his heart against him, how does God's love abide in him?

The Jerusalem brethren opened their hearts to one another because of the Spirit's work. They saw the needs of the many who had come to the Lord, so they sold their possessions to meet those needs. This principle was already established in the Old Testament, for example in Dt.15:7:

> If there is a poor man among your brothers in any of the towns of the land that the LORD your God is giving you, do not be hard-hearted or tightfisted toward your poor brother. (Dt.15:7, NIV)

Verses 10 and 11 (NIV):

> Give generously to him and do so without a grudging heart; then because of this the LORD your God will bless you in all your work and in everything you put your hand to. There will always be poor people in the land. Therefore I command you to be openhanded toward your brothers and toward the poor and needy in your land.

These words, spoken by Yahweh in Israel's early history, were applied many centuries later in Acts 4 by the brethren of the Jerusalem church who opened their hands generously to one another, meeting the needs of the many thousands who had come to the Lord. Their open-heartedness is possible only by God's work because we cannot on the human level tell others to sell their possessions against their will. This would be doing things the human way and by human compulsion. But because of the Spirit's work, the people gave voluntarily and spontaneously.

The spiritual fruits that emerged among the brethren—oneness in prayer, the performing of miracles, the breaking of bread, the community of goods—were also tied to the teaching of the apostles:

> They devoted themselves to the apostles' teaching and to the fellowship, to the breaking of bread and to prayer. Everyone was filled with awe, and many wonders and miraculous signs were done by

the apostles. All the believers were together and had everything in common. (Acts 2:42-44, NIV)

Because of the apostles' teaching and God's powerful work, the people shared all things in common:

> [32] All the believers were one in heart and mind. No one claimed that any of his possessions was his own, but they shared everything they had. [33] With great power the apostles continued to testify to the resurrection of the Lord Jesus, and much grace was upon them all. [34] There were no needy persons among them. For from time to time those who owned lands or houses sold them, brought the money from the sales [35] and put it at the apostles' feet, and it was distributed to anyone as he had need. (Acts 4:32-35, NIV)

The community of goods comes out strikingly in the statement, "no one claimed that any of his possessions was his own." The passage has an interesting structure in which v.33 on the apostle's preaching is sandwiched between the two verses (v.32, v.34) on the community of goods.

As a result "there were no needy persons among them". Those who owned lands or houses would sell them and lay the proceeds at the feet of the apostles. They didn't recklessly toss the money to the crowds in Jerusalem but quietly placed the proceeds at the feet of the apostles, knowing that they will distribute the funds according to God's will. Even in the giving of possessions, everything has to be done properly by the leading of the Spirit and not by human zeal.

The church, a spiritual body

Another lasting result of Pentecost is the formation of a body of believers, the church. If we don't know what it means to love our neighbor as ourselves, we will never grasp the nature of the New Testament church. For years I struggled to understand what is the nature of the New Testament church, and made no headway until I began to think more deeply on the command "love your neighbor as yourself."

Paul's concept of the church can be reconstructed from his letters. His letters are said to be "occasional letters" in the sense that each was written to a particular assembly for a specific purpose; these are not systematic writings on subjects such as the church. Hence we need to find statements here and there in his writings that teach about the church. Fortunately, his teaching on the church, the body of Christ, is concentrated in a few places such as 1 Corinthians 12.

After I had spent years looking into Paul's teaching of the church, one day it dawned on me that today we don't have a church that Paul envisages unless we dilute the meaning of *church* into some abstract entity. But even if we arrive at an understanding of what is the New Testament church by studying 1 Corinthians 12, where can we find such a church today? From my observations, such a church does not exist today except in small teams or groups.

In Paul's teaching of the church, a key characteristic of the church is the role of the Spirit in the church, as seen in 1Cor.12:13-14:

> For by one Spirit we were all baptized into one body, whether Jews or Greeks, whether slaves or free, and we were all made to drink of one Spirit. For the body is not one member but many. (NASB)

In the next two verses (vv.15,16), Paul gives an interesting picture of the body in which a foot talks about a hand, and an ear talks about an eye. This picture makes no sense until we see how the members of a body relate to one another. It is within a body that *as yourself* gains its fullest meaning. If the tip of your finger is pinched by a door, your whole body will react with great agitation. You let out a cry, and your eyes start to tear. It's only a small finger, so why the scream? Yet the reaction is immediate: your other hand nurses the finger, your feet are stomping, your heart is throbbing, your complexion is changing. Your whole body reacts to the pain in one finger. That is truly *as yourself*.

Are we similarly moved when calamities happen to others? If someone gets hurt in a car accident, do we say "poor brother" or "poor sister" and then move on? This is like a body that doesn't react when a finger gets hurt. If my reaction to your plight is minimal, then I don't regard you *as myself*, and I don't see you as me.

Where in the church today do we see the kind of interrelationship that Paul talks about? When Paul says that a foot or an ear is no less a part of the body than a hand or an eye, is he exaggerating what God intends for the church? Paul is not exaggerating. If you drop something on your toe, your whole body reacts, for the toe is connected to the rest of the body through the nervous system. The nervous system of the church is the Holy Spirit through whom we are baptized into one body (1Cor.12:13).

The people of the world get excited over human ties. Football and hockey fans jump up and down when there is a goal. When I was on a flight from Montreal to Vancouver, the plane stopped in Calgary. We all disembarked and walked to the transit lounge where a television monitor was showing a hockey game between Canada and the United States. I wasn't as interested in the hockey game as in the fervor of the spectators. Whenever Canada scored a goal, there would be wild celebration as if the fans had scored the goal themselves. But when the Americans scored, there would be dead silence or groaning.

I am impressed that hockey fans have a greater sense of identification with each other than Christians among themselves. When something good happens to you, does the church rejoice? When you are hit with a calamity, does the church feel your pain? There may be a word of sympathy, but is it heartfelt? Am I exaggerating when I say there is no church today of the New Testament kind whose members are bonded to each other by the Spirit such that what happens to you happens to everyone?

Unity in the Spirit

"Love your neighbor as yourself" is possible only by the work of the Spirit. Without the Spirit, you can love to a certain extent but not *as yourself*. It also means that salvation cannot be attained without the Spirit. The same can be said of the New Testament church: without the Spirit, the church becomes a mere organization. It may be an efficient organization but the world already has too many organizations. Without the unity of the Spirit, what we will have is an organization with an ideology, not a New Testament church whose members love one another as themselves.

Another aspect of New Testament teaching that we often miss is the concept of *in Christ*. We are in Christ because we have been baptized by one Spirit into one body (1Cor.12:13)—namely, into the body of Christ—and we are now members of the body. This unity is not an abstract ideal but something that can be practiced. Many other aspects of New Testament teaching will likewise remain abstract to us until we understand the principle of loving the neighbor as ourselves.

Since we are slow to understand spiritual things, Paul explains the concept of "in Christ" by means of the parallel concept of "in Adam," which is our human identity on the physical level. Perhaps it is this that unites Canadians over their hockey team, widely viewed as the best in the world. Canadians are proud of, and identify with, their hockey team. Common identity in Adam has various manifestations, for example, racial identity. But by the work of the Spirit, we have a common identity in Christ.

In giving, we receive

Even on the spiritual plane there is a "carnal" aspect: carnal in the specific sense of being easily understood even by the carnal person. For example Luke 6:38 says, "Give, and it will be given to you," which even a carnal man can understand, for when you give, you not only receive but receive more than you have given. In giving to others, you are giving back to yourself but with one difference: it comes back to you with interest. This striking principle is possible because God wants you to know that when you love your neighbor as yourself, you are also loving yourself. This also applies to forgiveness: If you forgive, you will be forgiven; if you don't forgive, you won't be forgiven (Mt.6:14-15).

God sees every person you encounter as an extension of yourself even though you may not see it that way. When you give to the other person, you will receive back because he is *as yourself*. But if you hold something back, you will lose it because you have not given it to yourself in the other person. This way of thinking requires the renewal of the mind! We need to think God's thoughts for His thoughts are higher than our thoughts. God sees the other person as being me. If I don't forgive, I won't be forgiven. If I forgive, I will be forgiven. If the $10 note in my pocket remains in my pocket, I will lose it at the judgment. But if I put it into your pocket, I will gain it and much more (Lk.6:38). If I save my life for myself, I will lose it (Mk.8:35, Lk.9:24).

Some will say, "Don't bother me with your problems. I want to enjoy life, so leave me in peace. If you talk to me about your problems, it will take up my time, which means I lose a part of my life." But it is in giving that I receive. The time I spend watching television is lost as far as eternity is concerned, but the time I spend with you in order to help you is the time I have gained as far as eternity is concerned. That is a remarkable reversal of human thinking!

Giving is the way to gain treasure in heaven (Lk.18:22). This is hard for us to understand because in human logic, if you give away what you have, you will have nothing left. But in biblical teaching, you will keep it for all eternity. What you give is registered in heaven. In giving to others, you have given to yourself. But what you keep for yourself on earth, you will eventually have to leave behind.

Spiritual equations

When we see that what we do to others, we do to ourselves, our thinking will be reversed, and barriers will be torn down. When we read the Bible, we will see the spiritual mathematics behind this principle. Consider these three statements:

1. You shall love the Lord your God with all your heart
2. You shall love your neighbor as yourself
3. Love one another as I have loved you

Each statement is scripturally correct. When you reflect on them, you will see equations linking them. Loving your neighbor as yourself is to love him with all your heart. The third statement, "as I have loved you," brings Christ into the picture and raises the standard for "love one another" and "love your neighbor". Hence we see a link between "as I have loved you" and "with all your heart" and "as yourself," since all these express total self-giving love. The first statement, "you shall love the Lord your God," is seen in the fact that what you do to your neighbor, you do to yourself and above all to God, who is hidden in the neighbor.

Another equation is that *God loves us as Himself.* This remarkable principle is found in Deuteronomy 32:10 (NASB):

> He found him in a desert land,
> And in the howling waste of a wilderness;
> He encircled him, He cared for him,
> He guarded him as the pupil of His eye.

God found Israel in the wilderness and cared for him, even protecting him as the pupil of His eye. Just as the body reacts over a hurt finger, so God regards Israel as the pupil of His eye, the most sensitive part of the body. One grain of sand can irritate the eye. This shows the extent of God's care for you: you are as dear to Him as the pupil of His eye.

We see this also in Psalm 17:8 ("Guard me as the apple (pupil) of your eye") and Zechariah 2:8 ("He who touches you touches the apple of His eye"). God's love for us is seen in His deep sensitivity to what happens to us. Whatever happens to His people happens to God in a profound way. He cares about our needs and sufferings, for in all the afflictions of His people, God was afflicted (Isaiah 63:9).

What "as I have loved you" means to us: four points

The first point: When Jesus says "love one another as I have loved you" (Jn.15:12), he is speaking as one who has done the very thing he tells us to do. As a sinless offering for our sake, he himself fulfilled the law summed up in loving the neighbor.

Second, "as I have loved you" sets the high standard for the way we love one another. The words "as I have loved you" bring out a love that is total and self-giving, and exemplified by how Jesus loved us and gave himself for us (Gal.2:20).

Third, "as I have loved you" brings out the truth that Jesus loves me every moment of every day. His love for me is ongoing. No member of a body is meant to be a part of the body only part-time. It must always be connected to the body if it is to be a part of a living body. Because I am in Christ and united to him by the Spirit, I live in the confidence of his love for me every moment of every day.

Fourth, "as I have loved you" expresses Jesus' total identification with us. This identification is seen in other statements such as "he who receives you receives me" (Mt.10:40) and "he who rejects you rejects me" (Lk.10:16). The identification extends even to the least of his brethren (Mt.25:31-46, the parable of sheep and goats). Some Christians think that Christ identifies more strongly with church leaders or spiritual people, but the fact is that whatever is done to the least of his brethren is done to him.

How God and Jesus identify with us: five points

We now summarize in five points the scriptural evidence for God's and Jesus' identification with us. This will overlap with some of the points in the preceding section. Because of this identification, when we love our neighbor as ourselves, we love God and Christ. The following is not exhaustive but merely serves to bring out some important truths.

1. The image of God. What I do to my neighbor is done to God because my neighbor bears the image of God by reason of creation and redemption (Gen.1:27; Jms.3:9). God's image in man has not been eradicated but is seen in man in its full glory (1Cor.11:7).

2. What we do, or fail to do, to the least of the brethren, we do or fail to do to Jesus himself (Mt.25:31-46, the parable of the sheep and goats). When Paul was persecuting Christians, he was persecuting Christ himself (Acts 9:4-5). What you do to a believer, you do to Christ, for the neighbor is identified with Christ. The identification is so strong as to bring out representation: "he who receives you receives me" (Mt.10:40) and "he who rejects you rejects me" (Lk.10:16).

3. There is total identification with Christ because we are *in Christ* (2Cor.5:17; Rom.12:5). What we do to someone who is in Christ is done to Christ himself.

4. Christ identifies with us because we are members of his body, the church (1Cor.12:27; Col.1:18; 1:24). We have been baptized by the Spirit into the body of Christ (1Cor.12:13), uniting us with him (Rom.6:4-5) and with one another. Our union with Christ is seen also in the fact that we are betrothed to him (2Cor.11:2).

5. The believer's physical body is the temple—the dwelling place— of God. What we do to the believer is done to God's dwelling and to God Himself (1Cor.3:16-17; 6:19-20). Hence we must honor the sanctity of the body. Harming one's own body (e.g. by glut- tony or drug abuse) is an action against God and His dwelling place.

A personal lesson

Early in my Christian life, I tried very hard to be a good Christian. For three years I tried with everything I had, yet I failed. In discourage- ment and despair, I knelt before God and said, "Lord, I am sorry I cannot live the life you have called me to, and I don't want to dishonor your name." Others thought I was a good Christian but the reality was that I couldn't live up to what God required of me. So I said, "Lord, the greatest favor I can do for you is for me to stop calling myself a Christ- ian and to leave the church all together." Then God graciously showed me that I was trying to live under the Law and to fulfill the commands in my own strength. After three years, by which time I had become ex- hausted and couldn't carry on, I handed my life over to the control of the Spirit, and soon everything changed.

I think everyone has to go through this learning process. I knew about the Spirit but I wasn't taught to depend on the Spirit moment by moment. But one day I opened my life to God and said, "Lord, please take control of my life," and He did. Things became very different after that. God honored my effort to live the best I could, and I experienced many miracles as did the Israelites in the wilderness. They weren't always an obedient people, yet they experienced many miracles by God's mercy. That is why I have been able to give my testimony in *How I Have Come to Know God*, which recounts many marvelous miracles of God.

God knew I had been trying hard to live the Christian life. When I finally surrendered to Him, He brought me out of the old covenant phase of my life and into the new covenant phase. It doesn't mean that all my spiritual issues were resolved in one flash: the Spirit continues to work in us. But on our part we cannot be passive; we still have to strive to enter by the narrow gate. But when we determine to follow God, He will give us strength even in the matter of fulfilling our commitment to Him.

I hope you can see the beauty of living in the fullness of the Spirit. The filling is not just about speaking in tongues or preaching the gospel but a whole new way of thinking. We relate to people in a new way and aim for a new society and community of God's people that shines as light in the darkness of the world.

Chapter 15

The Golden Rule and the
Renewing of the Mind

The Golden Rule

We begin this final chapter with what is commonly known as the Golden Rule, found in Matthew 7:12 (and Luke 6:31):

> So in everything, do to others what you would have them do to you, for this sums up the Law and the Prophets. (Mt.7:12, NIV)

The Golden Rule is also found in Chinese and Western ethical philosophy, but in negative form: "Don't do to others what you don't want others to do to you." Hillel the great rabbi is well known for his version of the Golden Rule: "What is hateful to you, do not do to your fellow human being" (*Shabbat*, 31a).

But Jesus gives the rule in its positive form: Do to others what you want others to do to you. This changes the fundamental character of the rule. The positive form includes the negative as a special case, but goes beyond the negative.

The negative is easy to fulfill. If you don't want others to criticize you, don't criticize others. If you don't want others to be rude to you, don't be rude. Refrain from doing what you don't want others to do to you. You will reap what you sow, so don't sow what you don't want to reap.

I consulted the multi-volume writings of the Ante-Nicene Fathers to see what they might have to say about the Golden Rule, but I was disappointed to see that when they refer to the rule, it is in the negative form again and again. I had a hard time finding references to the positive form as taught by the Lord Jesus. As for the Nicene and Post-Nicene Fathers: In the 29-volume *Ancient Christian Commentary on Scripture*, there are only two Fathers who refer to the Golden Rule in its positive form, but they are merely quoting Jesus' words without explaining what the rule means in practice.

Renewing the mind by practicing the Golden Rule

To live as true Christians, we need to be transformed in our thinking. Paul speaks of this as the renewing of the mind (Romans 12:2). It is not something that happens in one flash by a word of command but is attained by a spiritual method or process, namely, the practice of the Golden Rule with the help of the Spirit.

In what way does the application of the Golden Rule transform our thinking? When you are discouraged, what would you like others to do for you? Encourage you! Then you start thinking about doing for others what you want others to do for you. If you want someone to encourage you, go out and encourage someone. Then you will receive what you give.

Some people go down the drain spiritually because they are focused on themselves and their depression. When you are in such a situation, what would you like others to do for you? "I want someone to hug me and give me a shoulder to cry on." In that case, put your arms around someone who is discouraged. When your thinking is transformed, you will do for others what you want others to do for you. Even if they do nothing for you, you take the initiative to do something for them. You sow the seed of the fruit you are going to reap.

The beauty of this is that it pulls you away from self-love and teaches you to love others. If you say to yourself, "I feel lonely; if only someone could come and visit me," and yet you sit there wishing and wishing, you will only get more depressed because you are preoccupied with your own loneliness. If you want someone to visit you, go out and visit someone. You solve the problem of loneliness not by catering to it, but by visiting someone who is lonely. When two lonely people get together, neither will be lonely.

The outgoing character of the Golden Rule

Why doesn't Jesus give the Golden Rule as, "Do to others what you would do to yourself," since this is basically the substance of the rule? The problem is that there are many things you cannot do for yourself. If you are starving, this version of the Golden Rule won't work because you have no food to feed yourself. You don't have the means to help yourself, so you need someone to help you.

To understand the Golden Rule in its positive form as taught by Jesus, we must realize that it is focused on "others" with an outlook that forgets oneself. A transformed mind can forget oneself because it is confident that God will never forget His people (Isa.49:15-16). And didn't Jesus assure us that God will provide for our needs (Mt.6:25-34)? The Golden Rule helps us to focus on others without a trace of self-interest.

We do for others what they cannot do for themselves. In some situations, a person is powerless to help himself. If he is in prison, he cannot visit himself, but needs someone to visit him. If he is starving, he needs someone to give him food. The beauty of the Golden Rule is that it moves us from self-centeredness and guides us towards concern for others. Since we are no longer at the center of our own thinking, we can emulate the compassion seen in the parable of the sheep and the goats:

> For I was hungry and you gave me food, I was thirsty and you gave me drink, I was a stranger and you welcomed me, I was naked and you clothed me, I was sick and you visited me, I was in prison and you came to me. (Matthew 25:35-36, ESV)

The two stages of the Golden Rule

The first stage of the Golden rule goes something like this: You feel lonely and discouraged, so you deal with it by visiting the lonely and encouraging the discouraged. In the second stage, the focus is no longer on yourself because you are not the one who is hungry or thirsty or in need. So you imagine yourself in the position of someone who is hungry and thirsty, and ask, "If I were in his situation, what would I like someone to do for me?"

In the first stage, you are in a position of need, so you do for someone what you want others to do for you. In the second stage, you are not in a position of need, but move into someone else's situation, and do for him what he cannot do for himself.

Charles Colson, who was Special Counsel for President Richard Nixon, was put in jail for his role in the Watergate scandal. In prison he began to understand the needs of his fellow inmates, and how they longed for someone to care for them. Rejected by society, they were hoping that someone will show them concern. When Colson was released from prison, he remembered the pain he had experienced as an inmate, and started a prison ministry that has expanded to many parts of the world.

We could start with something less ambitious than a prison ministry, perhaps by identifying with someone in our household. If I am thirsty and wish that someone would make me a drink, I can say to myself, "I will make everyone a drink!" Instead of being unhappy that no one serves me, I will make everyone a drink. If everyone thinks like this, the next time around someone may make me a drink though this is not my motive. We have opportunities to learn self-giving love in the life of the body of Christ.

Going from the first stage to the second

In learning to care for others, initially we may be motivated by self-interest. I was watching a news report of a forest fire in California. There was an interview with a man who had helped save another person's house from being burned down. When asked why he saved the house, he said if another fire should threaten his own house in the future, his neighbors will come to his rescue. According to the report, the burning house was saved because of a collective effort to put out the fire. In fact most of the houses on the front line were saved. The man who was interviewed was motivated by, "If I do this for you, you will do the same for me."

Initially our helping the neighbor may be motivated by self-interest. Yet the self-interest can be transformed into love for the neighbor; he then becomes the "other" person who is in need but is not in a position to help himself. Your self-serving motive can be changed into a self-giving love, so that one day you will do more for others than anyone has ever done for you. We are reminded of the situation in which a person jumps into a river to save a drowning man without thinking of his own safety. He is putting his own life at risk because his survival is not guaranteed. If he drowns, he will have loved the other person more than himself.

Misusing the Golden Rule

Is the Golden Rule applicable in every situation? What about a situation of wrongdoing? If someone sees you shoplifting, you probably would not want him to report you to the police. Do we then apply the Golden Rule so that I don't report on you and you don't report on me? Only in a perverse way that makes us a band of thieves. The Rule works only for a certain type of person, for it is based on the Sermon on the Mount which is addressed to those who are pure in heart and hunger for righteousness.

If you commit a sin, what would you like others to do for you? Keep quiet about it or point it out? This is the cutting edge of the Golden Rule. It is not all strawberries and cream. If you stray from the Lord and commit more and more sins, what would you like others to do for you? Speak to you out of love? Give you a warning? Overlook your sins? How we apply the Golden Rule reveals a lot about ourselves.

Another situation: What if someone loves you more than God? Will you be happy if your wife loves you more than she loves God? Or your husband loves you more than he loves God? Or that he or she loves you and the Lord equally? At your wedding what would you want your fiancé or fiancée to promise you? To love you more than anyone else? Even more than God? Or do you say, "I want him or her to love the Lord more than me." You feel good for saying the right thing but what will happen when you are put to the test? If your fiancé or fiancée, or your husband or wife, goes on a missions assignment for the next six months, how will you take it?

The story of Xushu

I was wondering if there might be anyone in the secular world who wants others to love his country more than they love him. Then the story of Xushu of the Three Kingdoms period in Chinese history came to mind.

Xushu was one of several advisors to Liubei. Liubei, a warlord and the founder of the state of Shuhan, was not outstanding in many areas, but he had one excellent quality. Some people are outstanding in many areas but are ruined by one weakness, whereas others are not good in many areas but have one redeeming quality. The latter was true of Liubei. His redeeming quality was his ability and willingness to recruit talented people to advise him, and he owed much of his success to them. One of those he recruited was this Xushu, a gifted strategist. Liubei already had people like Guangong and Zhangfei who were more muscle than brains, so he was happy to find the right man in Xushu.

But Liubei's arch-enemy, Caocao, also had his eyes on Xushu. Caocao too was in search of talented people but his repulsive character had caused many to align themselves with Liubei who was a respected gentleman. So Caocao hatched a plan to lure talented people away from Liubei. He found out that Xushu's mother was living in his territory, so he forged a letter to Xushu allegedly written by his mother, telling him to visit her. Xushu received this letter, and because he was loyal to his mother, he rushed off to visit her out of filial piety.

In one of the moving incidents of the Three Kingdoms period, Liubei pleads with Xushu not to leave, even hanging on to his horse. But Xushu was determined to leave because he felt that his first duty was to his mother. But seeing Liubei's anguish, Xushu told him of a man named Zhuge Liang who could help him establish his kingdom. Then Xushu left.

He entered Caocao's territory, found his mother, and said to her, "You called for me, so I rushed back to you." She said, "I never called for you." Xushu replied, "But here's the letter you wrote me."

His mother said it was a forgery. Far from being happy to see her son, she reprimanded him: "You shouldn't have left Liubei because he is a good man whom China needs. You should have stayed with him to help him establish a just and righteous kingdom. Your priorities are wrong." Then she killed herself! Xushu was shattered, but he couldn't return to Liubei because he was trapped in Caocao's territory.

What commitment! His mother didn't want her son to love her more than the country, more than the kingdom, more than the welfare of the people. To show her commitment, she killed herself. How many Christians have a similar intensity of commitment? Earlier we asked, What do you want others to do for you? If you are a mother, do you want your son to love you more than God? Or equally with God? Or less than God?

Putting God first—nominally

I once interviewed a couple who were applying for the full-time ministry training. The husband was totally for God. I then asked the wife, "Please tell me the order of your priorities." To my surprise, it was her children first, her husband second, the church third—and of course the Lord above them all, nominally at least. It is easy to say that God comes first, but when the test comes, what will you do? The wife could not be accepted for the ministry training (much to her husband's disappointment) because we cannot allow anyone to serve God with wrong priorities. Again we see the cutting edge of the Golden Rule.

The "others" in the Golden Rule include first and foremost the people closest to us. Do I want them to love me more than God? If a church leader thinks like this, his priorities are upside down. I don't want anyone to love me more than God. When people become too devoted to me, I push them away. I don't want my wife to love me more than the Lord. I would suggest to her that she go out and serve God in some way. I can do the cooking and wash the dishes for myself from time to time. It would be a waste to have someone who is trained to serve God to do the cooking or the laundry for me when she could be meeting the spiritual needs of others. It would be self-centered of me to have her look after me while others are being denied the encouragement and teaching she could give them.

We want people to love us because we want to possess them. Parents often do this with their children. It is the demands of those closest to us—father or mother, son or daughter, brother or sister, husband or wife—that make it hard for us to obey the command to love the neighbor who is in need. But if we teach our children to love God first and foremost, this won't weaken our love for one another but will strengthen it.

Hate our family?

The Lord Jesus says in Luke 14:26:

> If anyone comes to me and does not hate his own father and mother and wife and children and brothers and sisters, yes, and even his own life, he cannot be my disciple. (ESV)

This verse sticks in our throats like a fish bone because of the word *hate*. But we mustn't run away from it, for when Jesus uses a strong word like *hate*, there must be a good reason for it. We find the word objectionable and wonder why loving the neighbor must exclude loving those closest to us such as husband, wife, father, mother, children. The fact remains that we need to deal with the word *hate*. What are we to do with it? Water it down? Many commentaries understand "hate" to mean "love less" and they quote Mt.10:37 for support: "Whoever loves father or mother more than me is not worthy of me."

But the absence of *hate* in Mt.10:37 does not remove *hate* from Lk. 14:26. If you look up the Greek word for *hate* or its Hebrew equivalent, you cannot evade the fact that *hate* really means hate and not "love less." I have confirmed this by consulting several dictionaries, including BDAG for Greek and BDB for Hebrew.

A principle of exegesis is to see how a writer uses the same word elsewhere in his own writings. Luke uses "hate" several times and in no instance does it mean anything less than hate. Examples include Luke 1:71 (we are saved from our enemies and those who hate us); 6:22 (blessed are you when men hate you); 6:27 (do good to those who hate you); 19:14 (the king's subjects hated him). The BDAG lexicon defines the Greek word for "hate" in these verses as *hate, detest, abhor.*

In Luke 14:26, "hate" is in the present continuous tense; hence it is an ongoing hate and not a one-time hate. The verse says that the disciple is to hate his own life, which accords with Jn.12:25 (he who hates his life will keep it to life eternal) where the same word "hate" is used.

The fact that Mt.10:37 is a weaker form of Lk.14:26 does not negate or nullify Lk.14:26. Mt.10:37 cannot be taken to mean that it is permissible for us to love father or mother on the same level as the Lord. That interpretation is possible if all we had was Mt.10:37, but Lk.14:26 rules it out.

The word "less" has a relative or comparative meaning rather than an absolute meaning. If we love someone less than the Lord, how much less? Slightly less, somewhat less, or much less? All these fall within the range of the meaning of "less". On the other hand, "hate" is not a relative term but the diametric opposite of love. The comparative "love less" may apply in some situations, but there are other situations which force us to choose the one or the other, as in the case of a teacher I knew personally in China. One evening after work, God told him in a vision to go and preach the gospel. When he told his wife about it, she told him to choose between her and God, for he cannot have both. When he declared his choice for God, his wife told him to leave the house, for she considered that he hated her.

The Levites killed their brothers

In studying a New Testament passage, we often need to consider its Old Testament connection. The background of our discussion on "hate" is the story of the golden calf in Exodus 32:6ff, and in particular what the Levites did in that incident. Moses had just come down from a mountain when he saw a chaotic situation in which the whole nation of Israel was worshipping the golden calf. So Moses said to the nation, "Whoever is on the LORD's side, come to me!" (v.26) All the sons of Levi responded to the call and flocked to Moses. Then Moses told them that by Yahweh's command, each man was to "put his sword upon his thigh, and go back and forth from gate to gate in the camp, and kill every man his brother, and every man his friend, and every man his neighbor" (v.27, NASB). The love of one's neighbor is now expressed in a radical way. No guilty person was to be spared. Sure enough, that day about 3,000 men fell to the sword (v.28). The swords of the Levites were dripping with the blood of their closest relatives.

In the New Testament age, killing the neighbor with the sword is not something that we do literally. Yet a similar question arises: If you should stray from God, forsake your commitment, apostatize, and lead others astray, what would you like your neighbor to do to you?

In the story of the golden calf, we see radical commitment among the Levites. There is an early parallel to this when Abraham was about to kill his son Isaac as a sacrifice to God (Genesis 22). How much did Abraham love his son? With all his heart and all his soul. He would have gladly died in place of Isaac if God had allowed it. He would have sacrificed himself at the altar if it meant his son could live. Isaac was young and had a future ahead of him, but Abraham was more than 100 years old. But because it was Abraham and not Isaac whom God was testing, it had to be Isaac who was to be offered. Abraham loved Isaac with all his being but he loved God even more.

Now we see what "hate" really means. At the very least, it includes loving God more than anyone else. How much more? To the extent that an observer would take your actions for God as hating the other person. When the Levites were killing their loved ones in obedience to Yahweh's command, in a real sense they were hating them. The Levites didn't just say to them, "I'll let you off this time, so don't do it again". Deuteronomy 33:9 says that each Levite "disowned his brothers and ignored his children".

Because 3,000 idol worshippers were killed, the rest of the nation was spared further disaster. Some commentators have noted that 3,000 out of two million people is not a high percentage.

By what they had done, the Levites ordained themselves into God's service and became the tribe of priests. Because of their commitment, they were sanctified: "Today you have been ordained for the service of the LORD" (Ex.32:29 ESV; HCSB has "dedicated to the LORD"). The Lord bestowed on them the blessing of the ministry. The Levites are the special servants of Yahweh God, for they have proven their commitment and faithfulness.

Similarly in Luke 14:26, your commitment to God establishes you as a disciple and you are ordained into the ministry of the kingdom of God. Some have noted that the 3,000 killed by the Levites are equal in number to the 3,000 added to the kingdom at Pentecost (Acts 2:41). The former were killed by the Levites; the latter came to life through the new Levites, the disciples of the Lord, since Christians are the new Levites: "He has made us a kingdom, priests to his God and Father" (Rev.1:6).

Will we respond to the call, Who is on the Lord's side? We are afraid to be extreme or radical. But if you go along with the crowd, you will be no different from the others. On the other hand, a radical person will stand out from the crowd and draw their attention.

Jesus says that the world hates us, and this is despite our love for the people of the world. But does the world really hate a philanthropist who cares for others? The world doesn't hate people who give to charity, but it hates those who love God and man radically and uncompromisingly. The world tolerates religion when it suits its purposes, but opposes those who put God and Christ above everyone else. Jesus says, "Everyone will hate you because of me" (Mk.13:13; also Mt.10:22; Jn.15:18; 17:14). We want to be liked, not hated, but Jesus says that if we are truly his disciples, we will be hated.

There is a remarkable incident from the Spring and Autumn period of China's history (8th to 5th century BC). There was an official by the name of Shi Que who lived in the state of Wei. He was a *daifu*, a high official. He had a son named Hou who conspired with Zhou Xu to assassinate a duke. When Shi Que found out about the plot, he had his son executed! From this incident comes the Chinese saying, *da yi mie qin* (to uphold righteousness above the welfare of one's own family). Executing a son for his crimes is rare in practice, not only in China but in the history of the world. This makes the incident of the Levites in Exodus 32 all the more remarkable when we take into account the vast scale of the killing.

A remarkable paradox

But if we live under the lordship of Jesus and obey his teachings in total commitment, we will experience a remarkable paradox: In hating our loved ones and in loving God above all, God's love will empower us to love them on a whole new level: the spiritual level. He will pour into our hearts a divine love (Rom.5:5) that carries a new quality and a new intensity. Far from loving them the less, we will love them the more, *with God's own love.* Many Christians have experienced this paradox and know it is real. It is related to the principle that we will lose what we cling to in carnal love. But if anyone hates his own life—and those who are dear to him—he will keep it for eternity (Jn.12:25; Mt. 10:39; 16:25).

A closing thought

Jesus gave himself *for* us. Note my emphasis on the word *for*. Jesus also uses *for* when he says, "Greater love has no one than this, that he lay down his life for his friends" (Jn.15:13). The word *for* is seen in many other verses which speak of Jesus' self-giving love for us: Gal.1:4 ("he gave himself for our sins"); 2:20 ("the Son of God who loved me and gave himself for me"); Titus 2:14 ("he gave himself for us"); Eph.5:25 ("as Christ loved the church and gave himself up for her"); 1Tim.2:6 ("he gave himself as a ransom for all").

For a time I was troubled by the word *for* because it seems to be inadequate. To explain what I mean, there is a television commercial about a father who worked hard for many years to give his family a better life. He worked so hard for his daughter's future that he was basically absent from her life, even missing her graduation ceremony because he was too busy doing things *for* her. For many years the daughter longed for her father's company more than all the good things he was providing *for* her.

Jesus does everything *for* me, but what I really want is Jesus himself. The "for me" is fine up to a point, but what I really want is Jesus himself and not just his salvation. I don't understand those who just want to be saved, for if we don't have Jesus, what is the point of being saved? It is wonderful to have gifts such as effective preaching, speaking in tongues, and healing, but the Lord is far more important.

For a time I was searching for a Bible verse which says that Jesus gave himself *to* me rather than *for* me. While many verses speak of his giving himself *for* me, it is hard to find one that says he gave himself *to* me. Then I saw something promising in Romans 8:32:

> He who did not spare his own Son but gave him up for us all, how will he not also with him graciously give us all things? (ESV)

Although the first half of the verse uses the word "for" rather than "to", the latter sense comes out in the second half which says that God and Christ had given us all things, which would include Jesus himself. This is strengthened by the word "also" which has the effect of explaining the first half of the verse (Jesus is given for us) by means of the second half (God and Jesus have given us all things). The words "with him" express Jesus' participation "with" God in the giving of all things, Jesus included. What comes out is that Jesus gave himself to me, which corresponds to the way I feel about him. To gain Christ, I cheerfully accept the loss of all things. But my commitment cannot be complete unless I enter into the intimate relationship with him as described in John 15, in which he gives himself to me, and I to him.

We are called to love God with our whole being and our neighbor as ourselves, which in practice means to love our neighbor more than ourselves. Our thinking must be centered on others, having the mind of Christ by the work of the Spirit. But our love for the neighbor, even our dearest ones, must never exceed—or even equal—our love for God, the Father of Jesus Christ. God is the ultimate source and object of all true love. He is the fountain of love from which commitment springs forth.

— END —

Scripture Index

Mt 10:37	204, 205	Mark 14:61-62	135	John 7:17	13
Mt 10:39	78	Mark 16:18	153, 154	John 7:38	176
Mt 10:39; 16:25	208	Luke 1:53	47	John 7:38-39	184
Mt 10:40	194	Luke 1:71	205	John 8:12	74
Mt 11:5; 19:21	42	Luke 4:18	47, 48	John 10:10	78
Mt 26:11	42	Luke 4:18; 6:20	42	John 10:11	157
Mt 11:19	90	Luke 6:20-25	43, 44	John 10:26-27	74
Mt 12	123	Luke 6:24-25	48	John 11:40	141
Mt 12:28	152	Luke 6:31	197	John 12:8	42
Mt 12:48	156	Luke 6:38	191, 192	John 12:23-25	75
Mt 12:50	72	Luke 6:43-44	118	John 12:24	85
Mt 13	32	Luke 7:22	48	John 12:25	79, 205, 208
Mt 13:13-15	31	Luke 7:22; 14:13	42	John 12:26	74
Mt 16:13,17	135	Luke 7:34	90	John 12:40	32
Mt 16:24	74	Luke 8:10	32	John 12:46	74
Mt 16:25-26	79	Luke 8:21	72	John 12:48	175
Mt 16:26	49, 78	Luke 8:56	94	John 13:34-35	157
Mt 19:16-22	182	Luke 9:24	192	John 14:6	131
Mt 19:17	108	Luke 10:16	194	John 14:15-17	72
Mt 19:19	163, 165	Luke 10:25-37	156, 180	John 14:16-17	73
Mt 19:19; 22:39	161, 163	Luke 10:27	161, 162, 163, 165	John 15	209
Mt 19:21	42			John 15:12	154, 193
Mt 19:21-22	47	Luke 11:4	122	John 15:13	208
Mt 19:23-24	150	Luke 11:22	123	John 15:13-15	62
Mt 19:27	155	Luke 11:23	103	John 15:14	92
Mt 21:21	171	Luke 11:52	113	John 15:17	153
Mt 22:37	6	Luke 12	24	John 15:18	207
Mt 22:39	154, 163, 164, 166	Luke 12:16-21	48	John 17:3	16
		Luke 12:20-21	49	John 17:14	207
Mt 23	116	Luke 12:32-34	50	John 20:17	16
Mt 25:31-46	194	Luke 14:12-14	50	Acts 2:4-12,45	186
Mt 25:35-36	199	Luke 14:21; 16	42	Acts 2:22	136
Mt 25:40	92	Luke 14:26	204, 205, 207	Acts 2:24,31,36	138
Mt 26:52	55			Acts 2:36	57
Mt 26:63-64	135	Luke 14:33	50, 182	Acts 2:41	207
Mt 28:10	92	Luke 16:8,9	40	Acts 2:42-44	188
Mark 3	123	Luke 16:11-14	51	Acts 2:44-45	68
Mark 3:35	72	Luke 16:12	52, 53	Acts 3	97
Mark 4:12	32	Luke 18:19	108	Acts 4	187
Mark 7:36; 8:26	94	Luke 18:22	192	Acts 4:32	68
Mark 8:35	192	Luke 18:22-23	50	Acts 4:32-35	188
Mark 10:21	42	Luke 18:24-25	53	Acts 5:32	73
Mark 11:22-23	171	Luke 19:2	54	Acts 9:4-5	194
Mark 12:31	161, 166	Luke 22:27	74	Acts 16:27,30-31	81
Mark 12:31-33	163, 164	Luke 23:46	6	Acts 16:31	80, 82
Mark 12:43	42	John 1:12	26, 73	Acts 20:26-27	79
Mark 13:13	207	John 6:38,39,44	73	Acts 28:3-6	154
Mark 14:7	42	John 7:16,28,33	73	Acts 28:26	32

47425940R00127

Made in the USA
Middletown, DE
24 August 2017